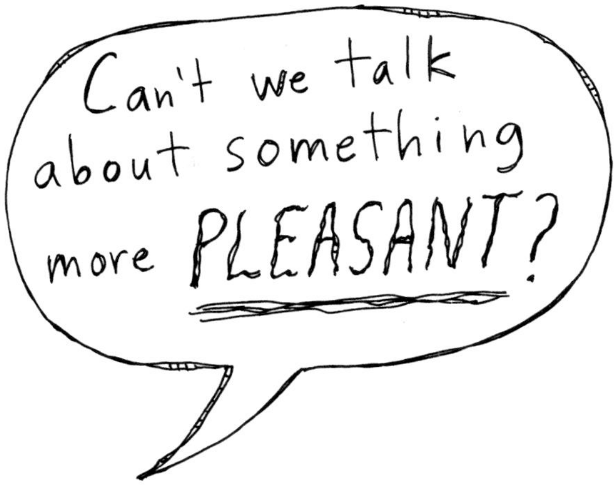
Can't we talk about something more PLEASANT?

BY THE SAME AUTHOR

What I Hate

A Friend for Marco

Too Busy Marco

Theories of Everything

The Party, After You Left

Childproof

Mondo Boxo

Proof of Life on Earth

The Four Elements

Parallel Universes

Unscientific Americans

Poems and Songs

Last Resorts

BLOOMSBURY
New York   London   New Delhi   Sydney

Published by Bloomsbury USA, New York

All papers used by Bloomsbury USA are natural, recyclable products made from wood grown in well-managed forests. The manufacturing processes conform to the environmental regulations of the country of origin.

LIBRARY OF CONGRESS CATALOGING-IN-PUBLICATION DATA HAS BEEN APPLIED FOR.

ISBN: 978-1-60819-806-1

First U.S. edition 2014

3 5 7 9 10 8 6 4 2

Printed and bound in China by C & C Offset Printing Co. Ltd.

To my parents,
George and Elizabeth

CONTENTS

What IS all this?
It's just a CONTENTS, George.
Stop getting nervous in the service.
Maybe I'll make some tea.
Use the tea bag on the counter.
It still has plenty of juice in it.
LIP-TON

INTRODUCTION

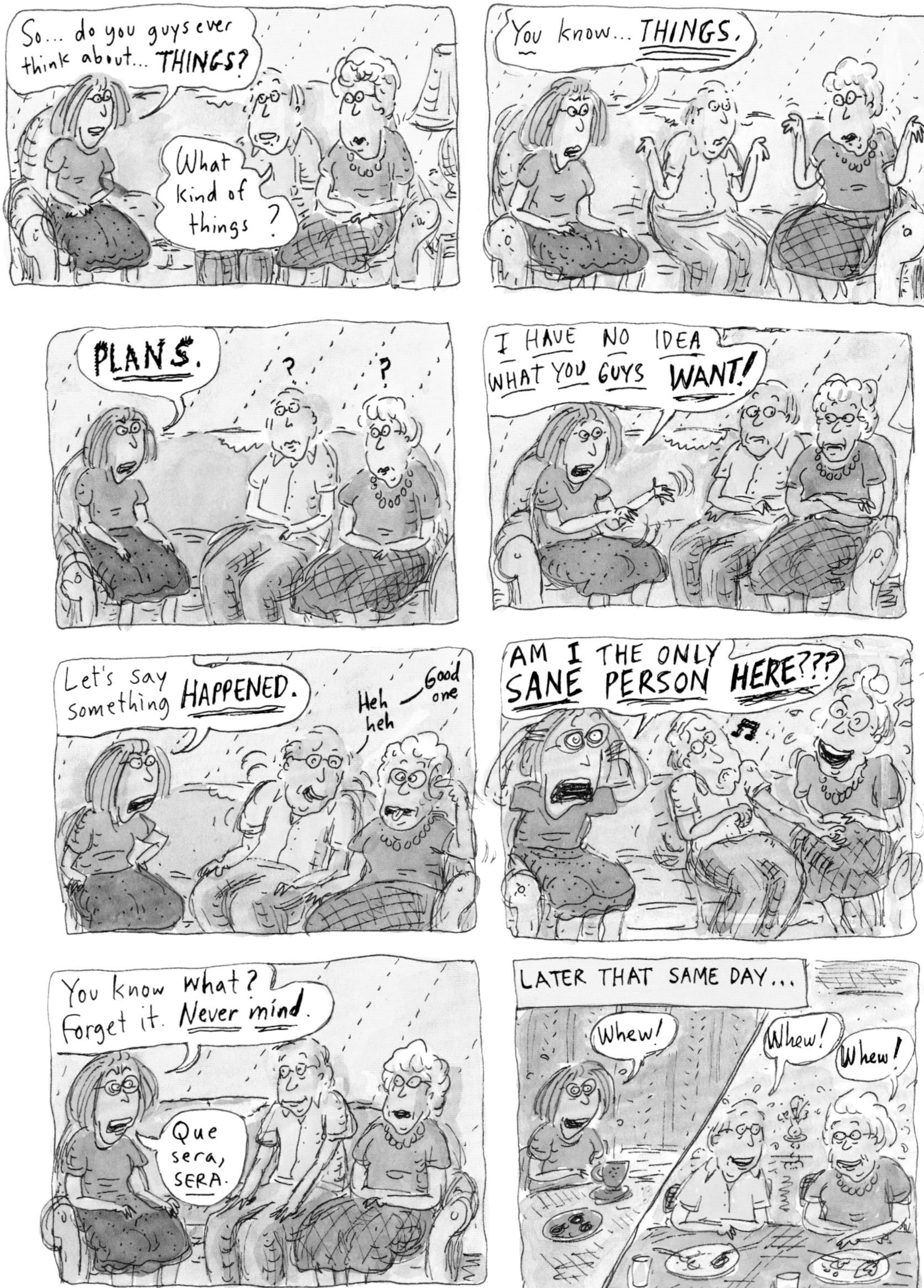
So... do you guys ever think about... THINGS?
What kind of things?
You know... THINGS.
PLANS.
?
?
I HAVE NO IDEA WHAT YOU GUYS WANT!
Let's say something HAPPENED.
Heh heh
Good one
AM I THE ONLY SANE PERSON HERE???
You know what? Forget it. Never mind.
Que sera, SERA.
LATER THAT SAME DAY...
Whew!
Whew!
Whew!

It was against my parents' principles to talk about death...

4

One day in the year 1940, an overhead lightbulb in my parents' apartment in Brooklyn burned out. My father had phobias about both changing lightbulbs and climbing even a small stepstool. Therefore, my mother climbed the stepstool and reached for the bulb. At the time, she was 6½ months pregnant.

Shortly thereafter, she began to hemorrhage. The doctor told her to stay in bed for the rest of the pregnancy. It didn't help. At 7½ months, she gave birth to a girl who died after a day. My aunt, the only relative from that time who is still alive, said, "She was perfectly formed, but blue." My mother nearly died too.

The cause of all this misery was a placenta previa. It had nothing to do with reaching for a lightbulb, even though whenever I heard the story of my almost-sister, "reaching" definitely took some of the blame. I heard this story frequently. It was part of "family lore."

THE FIRST BABY.

MY MOTHER REFERRED TO THE ENTIRE EPISODE AS "THAT MESS."

SHE IS BURIED IN A CEMETERY (MY AUNT TOLD ME), BUT I DON'T KNOW WHICH ONE.

MY PARENTS DIDN'T LIKE IT WHEN I ASKED QUESTIONS ABOUT HER.

I was quite aware that my parents had had tough lives - way, way tougher than mine.

You don't know what trouble IS!

I had heard the stories my whole life - about how their parents had come over from Russia at the turn of the century with NOTHING —

- about how my maternal grandfather had been an engineer in Russia, but how, between his inability to speak English and his being Jewish, he wound up barely being able to support five kids and his wife working as a presser in the garment district;

and how bitter and angry he was; and how my grandmother washed clothes for other people;

and how even **sadder** my father's family was: his mother was one of nine children.

Not only was she the only girl, but she was also the only one of her siblings to survive the Russian cholera epidemic.

Then, her father's throat got cut "from ear to ear" in a forest by "bandits."

I don't know what happened to her mother. But she came to New York, married my paternal grandfather, and had just one child, my father, by cesarean section in 1912...

...a horrible ordeal which involved, according to my mother, "opening her up from her neck to her you-know-what."

Between their one-bad-thing-after-another lives and the Depression, World War II, and the Holocaust, in which they'd both lost family —

it was amazing that they weren't crazier than they were.

Who could blame them for not wanting to talk about death?

Let's discuss a more pleasant subject.

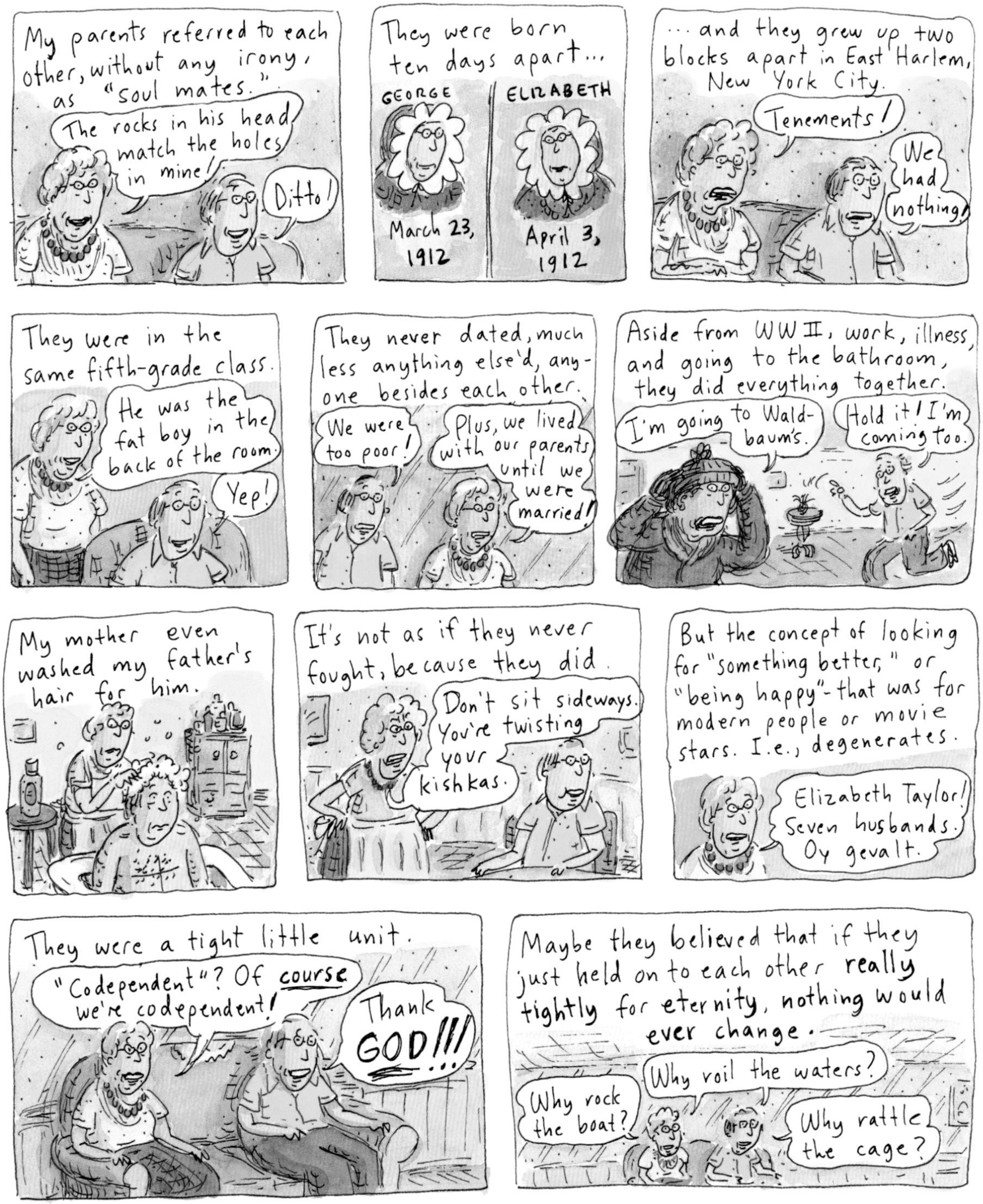

My parents referred to each other, without any irony, as "soul mates."
The rocks in his head match the holes in mine!
Ditto!
They were born ten days apart...
GEORGE
ELIZABETH
March 23, 1912
April 3, 1912
...and they grew up two blocks apart in East Harlem, New York City.
Tenements!
We had nothing!
They were in the same fifth-grade class.
He was the fat boy in the back of the room.
Yep!
They never dated, much less anything else'd, anyone besides each other.
We were too poor!
Plus, we lived with our parents until we were married!
Aside from WW II, work, illness, and going to the bathroom, they did everything together.
I'm going to Waldbaum's.
Hold it! I'm coming too.
My mother even washed my father's hair for him.
It's not as if they never fought, because they did.
Don't sit sideways. You're twisting your kishkas.
But the concept of looking for "something better," or "being happy"-that was for modern people or movie stars. I.e., degenerates.
Elizabeth Taylor! Seven husbands. Oy gevalt.
They were a tight little unit.
"Codependent"? Of course we're codependent!
Thank GOD!!!
Maybe they believed that if they just held on to each other really tightly for eternity, nothing would ever change.
Why rock the boat?
Why roil the waters?
Why rattle the cage?

① THE BEGINNING OF THE END

Two things about my childhood: ① I was an only child; and ② my parents were a lot older than other kids' parents.

As my parents and I moved inexorably into this "future," I became more and more aware that at some point, we were all going to have to deal with this **aging** thing.

And even when they really *were* a zillion, they—and I—never talked about "the future."

As my parents and I moved inexorably into this "future," I became more and more aware that at some point, we were all going to have to deal with this **aging** thing.

But they weren't asking for help, and I wasn't volunteering. In 1990, my husband, our three-year-old son, and I (pregnant with our soon-to-be-born daughter) moved out of the city to the suburbs of Connecticut where there was more space, and greenery, and good public schools. If doing right by our kids meant abandoning my then-78-year-old parents, so be it. The longer we were there, the more impossible schlepping into Brooklyn seemed. If they wanted to see us so damn much, let *THEM* make the trip!!!

Also, I **LOATHED** Brooklyn, which was where they still lived, in the same apartment in which I spent my unhappy childhood. The neighborhood was depressing, their apartment was depressing. Who needed it?

I had no nostalgia for the Carefree Days of Youth, because I never had them.

The "to-do" list of my childhood and adolescence would have looked like this:

① Do well in school.
② Practice piano.
③ Avoid contact with other children.
④ Be good.
⑤ Look up symptom in Merck Manual.
⑥ Do not die.

I hated that time of my life! Why would I ever want to return?!?

From 1990 to 2001, I had not set foot in Brooklyn ONCE. Denial, avoidance, selfishness, laziness, and the day-to-day busyness of my life (two little kids! cartoon deadlines! grocery shopping!) were all partly to blame. But really, I just didn't want to. Then, one day, out of the blue, I had an _intense need_ to go out to Brooklyn, to visit my parents. It was easy to remember the day because of the events that followed - September 9, 2001. A Sunday.

The taxi made its way into Brooklyn. Not Brooklyn Heights or Park Slope or even Carroll Gardens. Not the Brooklyn of artists or hipsters or people who made - and bought - $8.⁰⁰ chocolate bars. This was DEEP Brooklyn, the Brooklyn of people who have been left behind by everything and everyone. The Brooklyn of smelly hallways and neighbors having screaming fights and where no one went into Manhattan — "the city" — unless it was for their job at Drudgery, Inc.

We drove down Ocean Parkway, the benches, the six-story apartment houses... we were in my old neighborhood, then on my old block, and finally, there was the old building where I grew up and where my parents were still living.

The cab pulled up. I got out and entered the building, filled with dread, guilt, and a weird kind of claustrophobia.

Same plastic flowers in the alcove in the lobby

Same chair bolted to the floor, occupied by possibly the same tenant, still waiting for the mailman.

APTS. A–L

The mail room had a locked gate now. That was new.

Same elevator. Still slow. Same weird smell, too.

What awaited me???

Time to face the music.

So! You've come to check up on the OLD FOLKS.

My parents' names were Elizabeth and George.
They knew each other forever.

They got married on June 25, 1938.

I was born on November 26, 1954.

My father died on October 17, 2007.
My mother died on September 30, 2009.

What I noticed first was the level of

GRIME

What **IS** "grime"?

It's not ordinary dust, or dirt, or a greasy stovetop that hasn't been cleaned in a week or two. It's more of a coating that happens when people haven't cleaned in a *really long time*. Maybe because they're old, and they're tired, and they don't see what's going on. It covered everything:

The cookie jar...	...chairs...	...knickknacks...	...silverware...	...books...

One thing my mother always told me when I was growing up was:

You have to DUST! If you don't, the dust gets into all the *interstices* of the furniture and BREAKS IT ALL APART!!!

It was clear that she had stopped worrying about that.

15

If you pick up a sponge and start cleaning...

♫ Look at me! ♫

It's PERFECT DAUGHTER®!

... it will not necessarily be perceived as helpful.

The person you're trying to help might even feel insulted, or embarrassed.

Put that down.

What are you doing that for?

I want that exactly where it is.

Don't touch that.

Daddy and I are FINE.

Don't upset your mother.

I wasn't great as a caretaker, and they weren't great at being taken care of.

16

Two days later, those two big dumb towers of the World Trade Center - the same ones I had just registered from the taxi window - were improbably, inconceivably <u>GONE</u>.

I called my parents right after the second plane hit.

9/11/01

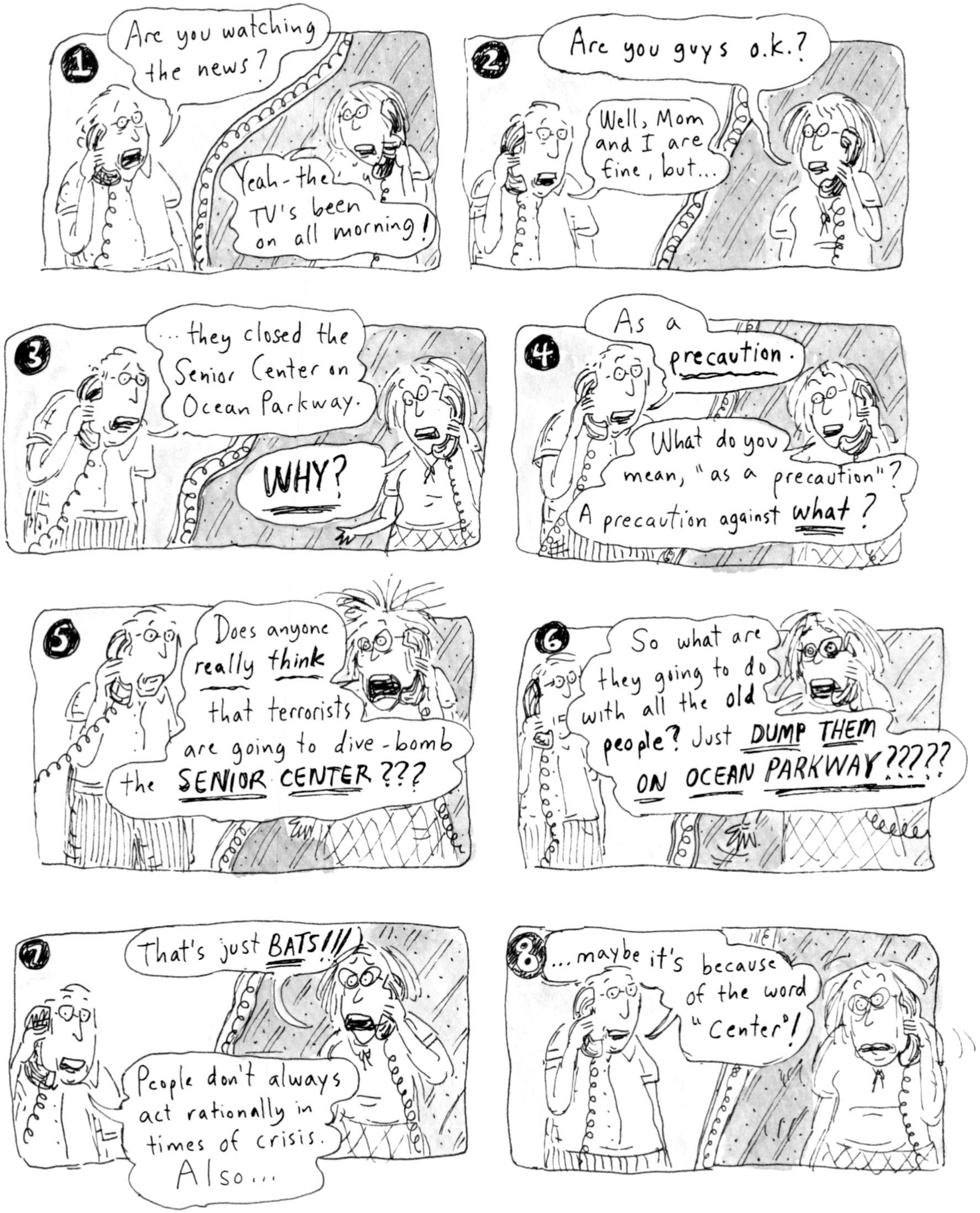

Are you watching the news?
Yeah-the TV's been on all morning!
Are you guys o.k.?
Well, Mom and I are fine, but...
...they closed the Senior Center on Ocean Parkway.
WHY?
As a precaution.
What do you mean, "as a precaution"? A precaution against what?
Does anyone really think that terrorists are going to dive-bomb the SENIOR CENTER???
So what are they going to do with all the old people? Just DUMP THEM ON OCEAN PARKWAY?????
That's just BATS!!!
People don't always act rationally in times of crisis. Also...
...maybe it's because of the word "Center"!

9/12/01

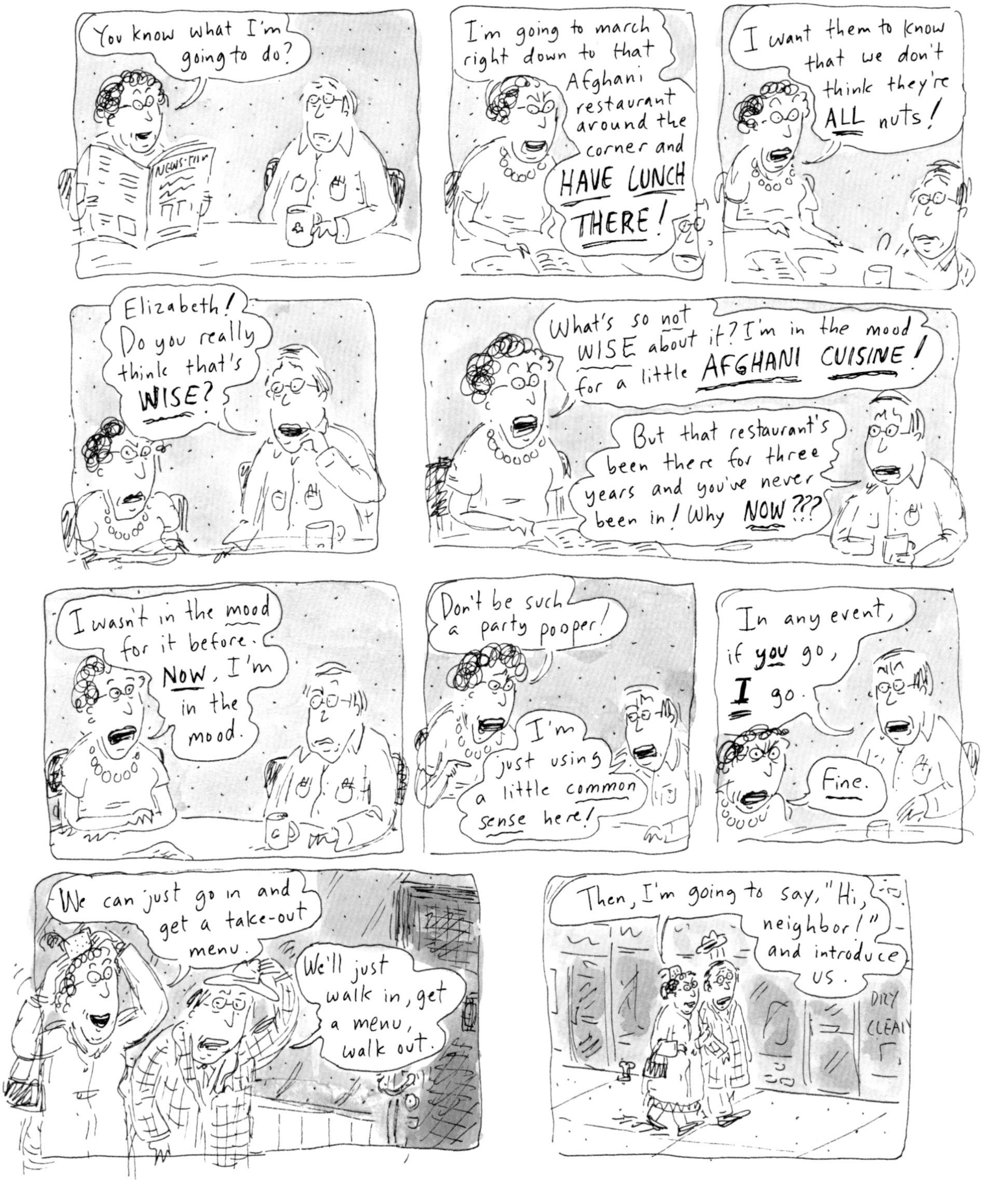

You know what I'm going to do?
I'm going to march right down to that Afghani restaurant around the corner and HAVE LUNCH THERE!
I want them to know that we don't think they're ALL nuts!
Elizabeth! Do you really think that's WISE?
What's so not WISE about it? I'm in the mood for a little AFGHANI CUISINE!
But that restaurant's been there for three years and you've never been in! Why NOW???
I wasn't in the mood for it before. NOW, I'm in the mood.
Don't be such a party pooper!
I'm just using a little common sense here!
In any event, if you go, I go.
Fine.
We can just go in and get a take-out menu.
We'll just walk in, get a menu, walk out.
Then, I'm going to say, "Hi, neighbor!" and introduce us.

After 9/11, things quickly returned to the usual routine, with my parents fighting their usual battles.

Bananas are disgusting.

Bananas are Nature's perfect food.

This was depressing, but also reassuring—at least to me.

Whatever marbles they ever had, I guess they still have.

Nevertheless, by 2002, they were 90, and it was hard not to notice that every time I came to see them, the grime had grown thicker...

COOKIES

...The piles of newspapers, magazines, and junk mail had grown larger...

...and they themselves had grown frailer.

I could see that they were slowly leaving the sphere of TV commercial old age—

• SPRY!
• TOTALLY INDEPENDENT!!
• JUST LIKE A NORMAL ADULT, BUT WITH SILVER HAIR!!!

—and moving into the part of old age that was scarier, harder to talk about, and not a part of this culture.

...600 calories a day, live till 140...

...cryogenically frozen head...

...kale...

...drink glass of vinegar a day, live FOREVER.

SOMETHING WAS COMING DOWN THE PIKE.

RETURN TO THE FOLD

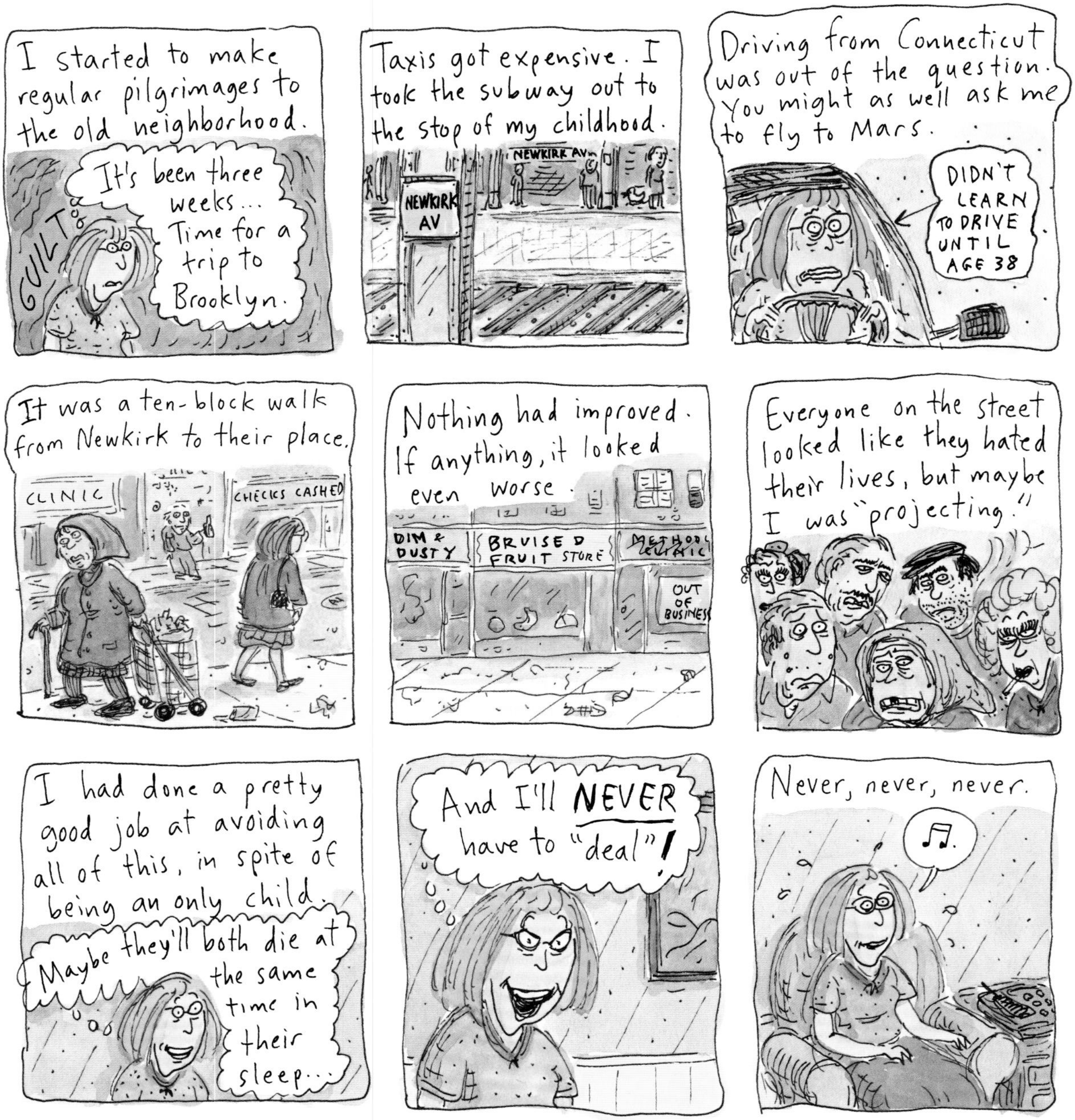

I started to make regular pilgrimages to the old neighborhood.
GUILT
It's been three weeks... Time for a trip to Brooklyn.
Taxis got expensive. I took the subway out to the stop of my childhood.
NEWKIRK AV
NEWKIRK AV
Driving from Connecticut was out of the question. You might as well ask me to fly to Mars.
DIDN'T LEARN TO DRIVE UNTIL AGE 38
It was a ten-block walk from Newkirk to their place.
CLINIC
CHECKS CASHED
Nothing had improved. If anything, it looked even worse.
DIM & DUSTY
BRUISED FRUIT STORE
OUT OF BUSINESS
Everyone on the street looked like they hated their lives, but maybe I was "projecting."
I had done a pretty good job at avoiding all of this, in spite of being an only child.
Maybe they'll both die at the same time in their sleep...
And I'll **NEVER** have to "deal"!
Never, never, never.

It was too hard-(time-consuming, expensive, and emotionally exhausting)- to visit them "in person" more than once every couple of weeks. But we spoke almost every day on the phone.

SHERLOCK HOLMES, M.D.

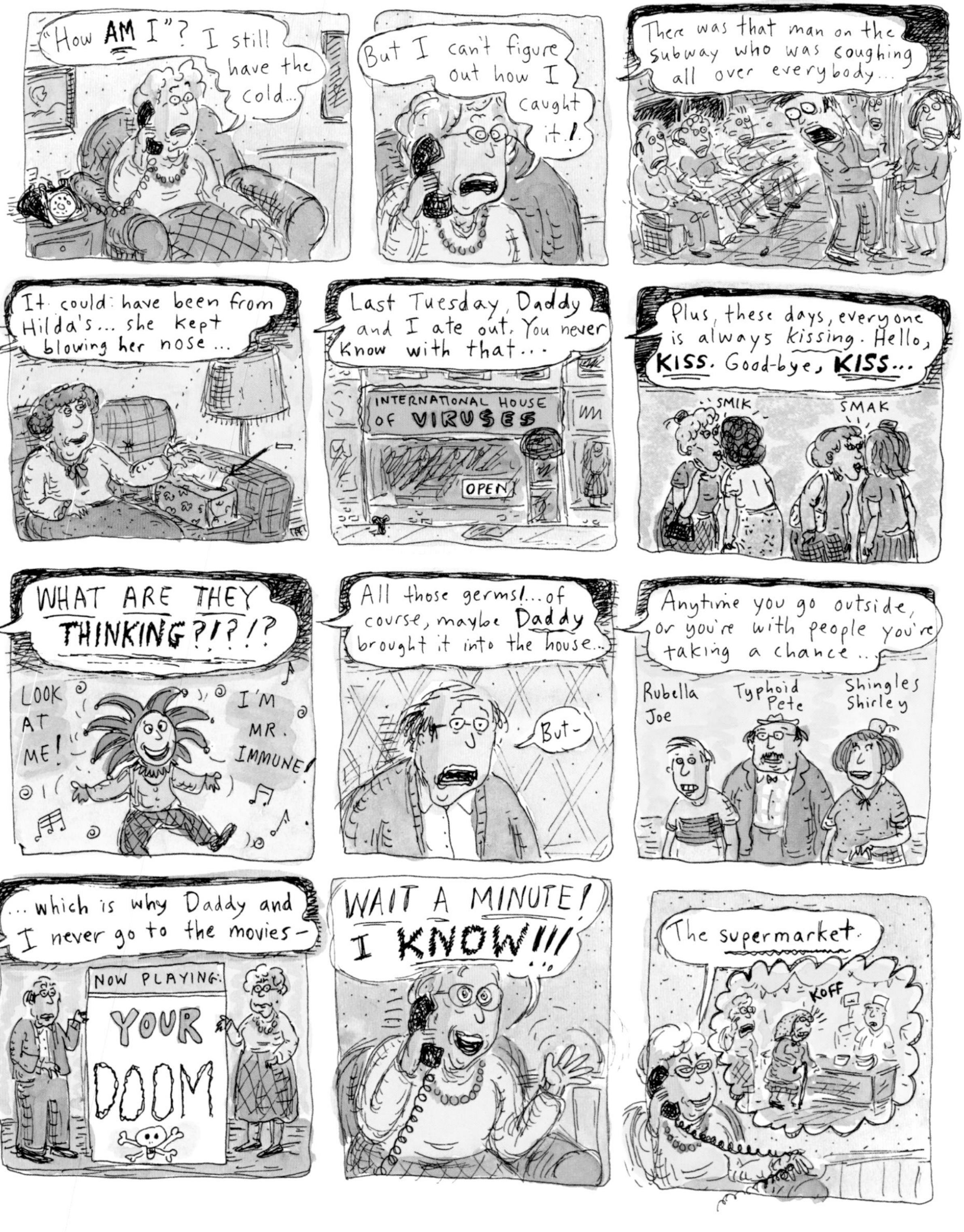

"How AM I"? I still have the cold...
But I can't figure out how I caught it!
There was that man on the subway who was coughing all over everybody...
It could have been from Hilda's... she kept blowing her nose...
Last Tuesday, Daddy and I ate out. You never know with that...
INTERNATIONAL HOUSE OF VIRUSES
OPEN
Plus, these days, everyone is always kissing. Hello, KISS. Good-bye, KISS...
SMIK
SMAK
WHAT ARE THEY THINKING?!?!?
LOOK AT ME!
I'M MR. IMMUNE!
All those germs!... of course, maybe Daddy brought it into the house...
But-
Anytime you go outside, or you're with people you're taking a chance...
Rubella Joe
Typhoid Pete
Shingles Shirley
...which is why Daddy and I never go to the movies-
NOW PLAYING
YOUR DOOM
WAIT A MINUTE! I KNOW!!!
The supermarket.
KOFF

A RARE SEX TALK

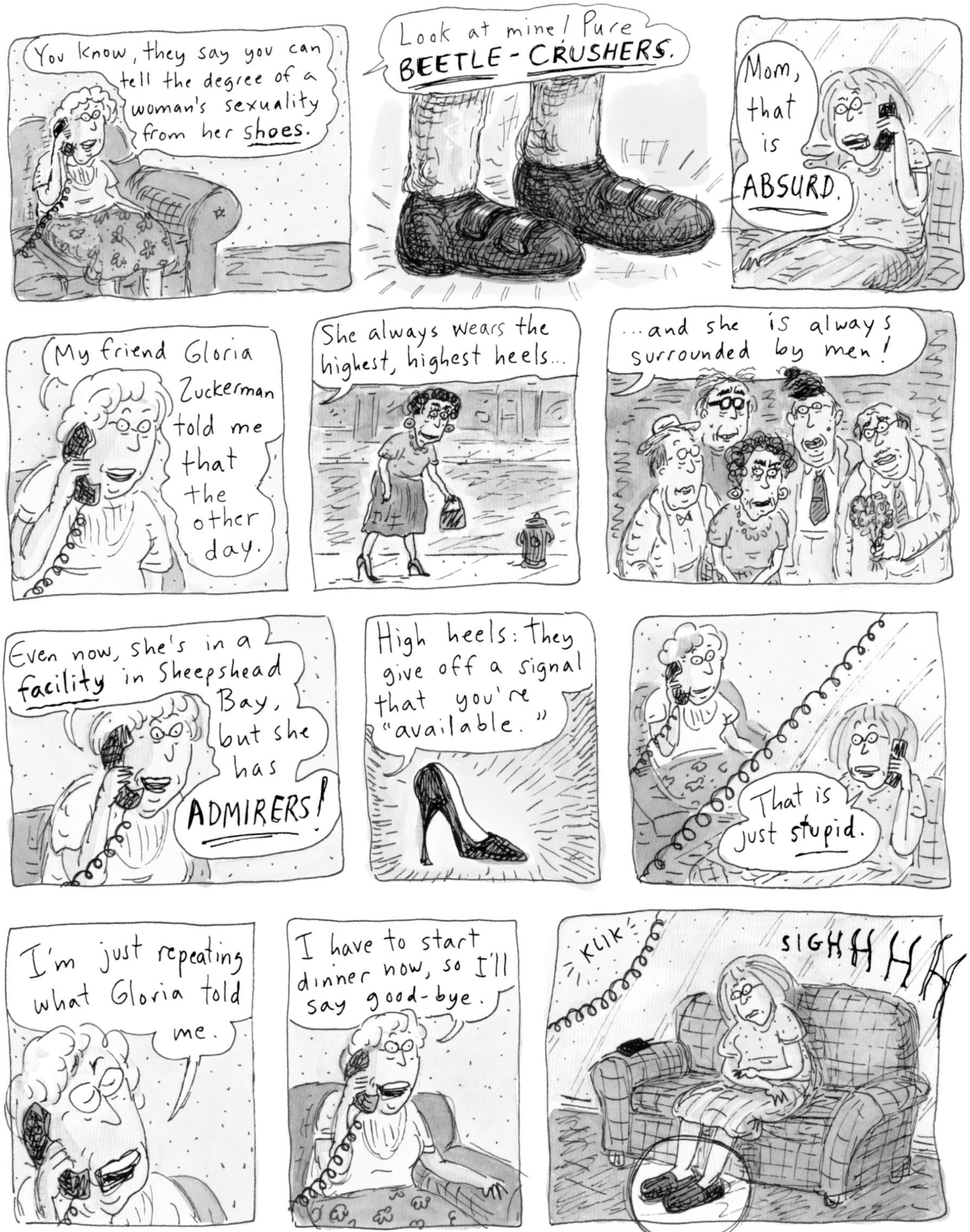
You know, they say you can tell the degree of a woman's sexuality from her shoes.
Look at mine! Pure BEETLE-CRUSHERS.
Mom, that is ABSURD.
My friend Gloria Zuckerman told me that the other day.
She always wears the highest, highest heels...
...and she is always surrounded by men!
Even now, she's in a facility in Sheepshead Bay, but she has ADMIRERS!
High heels: They give off a signal that you're "available."
That is just stupid.
I'm just repeating what Gloria told me.
I have to start dinner now, so I'll say good-bye.
KLIK!
SIGHHHH

SAFETY: 2003

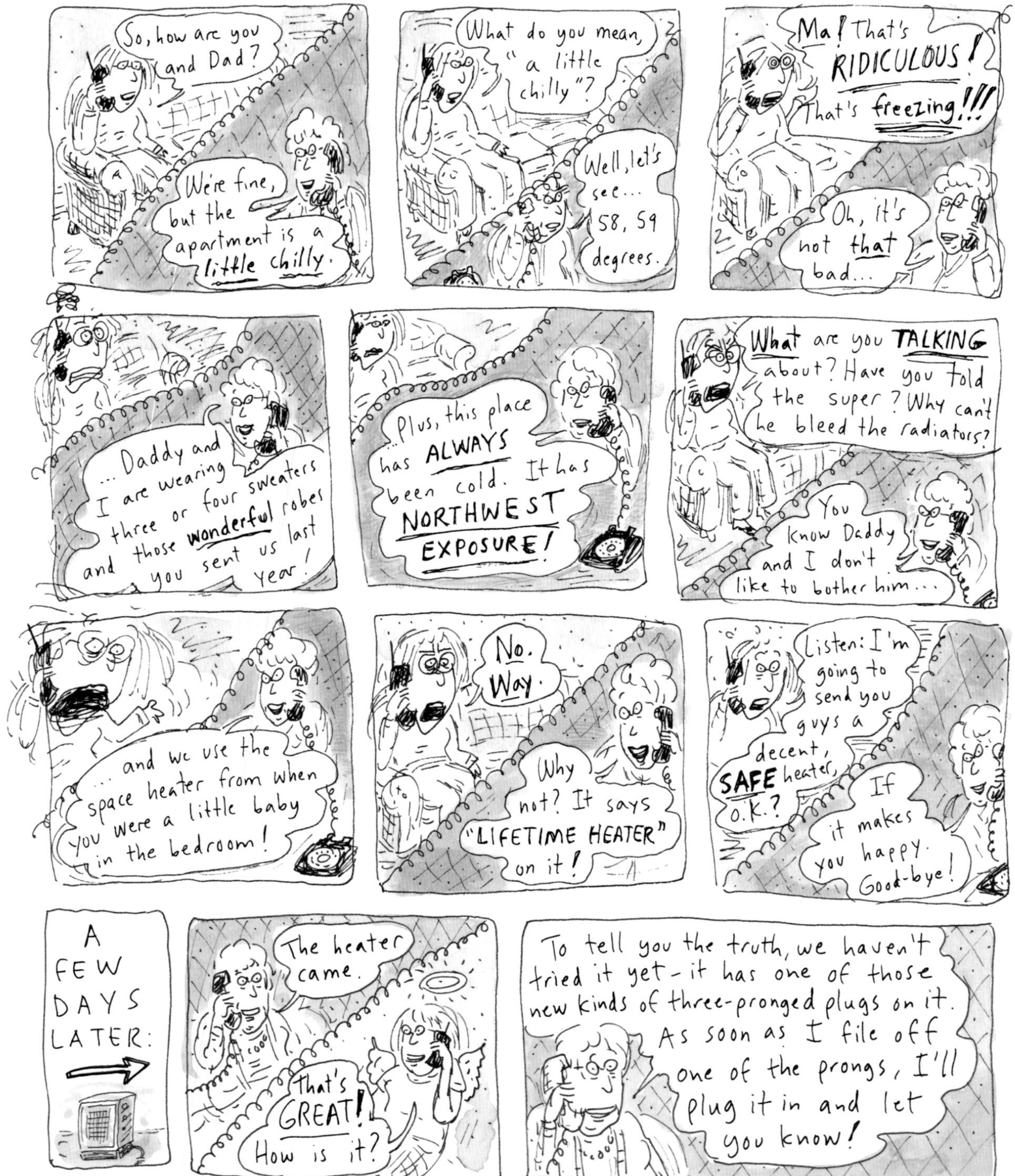

So, how are you and Dad?
We're fine, but the apartment is a little chilly.
What do you mean, "a little chilly"?
Well, let's see... 58, 59 degrees.
Ma! That's RIDICULOUS! That's freezing!!!
Oh, it's not that bad...
...Daddy and I are wearing three or four sweaters and those wonderful robes you sent us last year!
...Plus, this place has ALWAYS been cold. It has NORTHWEST EXPOSURE!
What are you TALKING about? Have you told the super? Why can't he bleed the radiators?
You know Daddy and I don't like to bother him...
...and we use the space heater from when you were a little baby in the bedroom!
No. Way.
Why not? It says "LIFETIME HEATER" on it!
Listen: I'm going to send you guys a decent, SAFE heater, O.K.?
If it makes you happy. Good-bye!
A FEW DAYS LATER:
The heater came.
That's GREAT! How is it?
To tell you the truth, we haven't tried it yet - it has one of those new kinds of three-pronged plugs on it. As soon as I file off one of the prongs, I'll plug it in and let you know!

Of course, there were ailments - the usual troubles that come when people get past a certain age. My mother's were mainly physical (high blood pressure, arthritis, digestive ailments with symptoms that would throw most people into a panic, but which my mother would just wait out) and my father's were mental (increasing senile dementia). Things were going downhill, but for many years, the decline was blessedly gradual.

My mother belonged to a Poetry Club. She also played classical piano in a group that, to all the members' amusement, was called Classical Pianists in Retirement: CPR.

Old age didn't change their basic personalities. If anything, it intensified what was already there.

My father chain-worried the way others might chain-smoke. He never learned to drive, swim, ride a bicycle, or change a lightbulb. He was not handy. I never saw him use the stove except to boil water for tea. Even using a simple toaster could become a challenge — and that was before he had senile dementia.

How do you know which one?

Now, let's see... You put the bread into one of these two compartments...

Do you put the bread in first?? Or do you press this little lever down first???

He was bad at opening packages, like cookies or cereal. You could tell which ones he'd tried to open, because they were always torn in some strange way, as if a raccoon had tried to get into them.

(Some of this incompetence was related to his chronic anxiety, I'm sure. What if he did it wrong?!?)

The wheel of DOOM, surrounded by "cautionary" tales of my childhood.

He had food anxieties galore. He didn't "believe in" eating uncooked apples. Drinking cold beverages appalled him. He routinely added warm water to cold juice out of the refrigerator to "kill the chill."

He was also obsessed with eating slowly. My mother ate very quickly. This was one of their big points of contention:

* an old college chum of his

Asking a person if they, or anyone in their family, was a "slow eater" was one of his favorite conversational openers.

In spite of all of these things, he was smart in other ways. He loved languages and had been a high school French and Spanish teacher. He also spoke Italian and Yiddish. He loved words and word origins.

And, more important, he was kind and sensitive. He knew that my mother had a terrible temper, and that she could be overpowering. She had a thick skin. He, like me, did not. She often accused my father of "walking around with his feelers out."

In many ways, my father and I were more alike than my mother and I. We were both only children, and less used to the constant emotional tumult between people than my mother, who was one of five. Also, we were both dilly-dalliers and easily distracted by, say, an interesting word, thereby missing the larger point of what was being said. He often kept me company when my mother was doing other stuff. We watched Twilight Zone together. I'm sure he thought it was dopey, but he knew I loved it, and that I was too scared to watch it alone.

He taught me an old-fashioned card game called Casino, and listened to me prattle on about the Beatles, which my mother had no patience with. He liked to walk. My mother couldn't— she had "bad feet." They certainly looked awful— all bunions and hammertoes and bulges and scary vein clusters. He and I sometimes walked to the local candy store for a malted or a grilled cheese. Even though I knew he couldn't really defend me against my mother's rages, I sensed that at least he felt some sympathy, and that he liked me as a person, not just because I was his daughter.

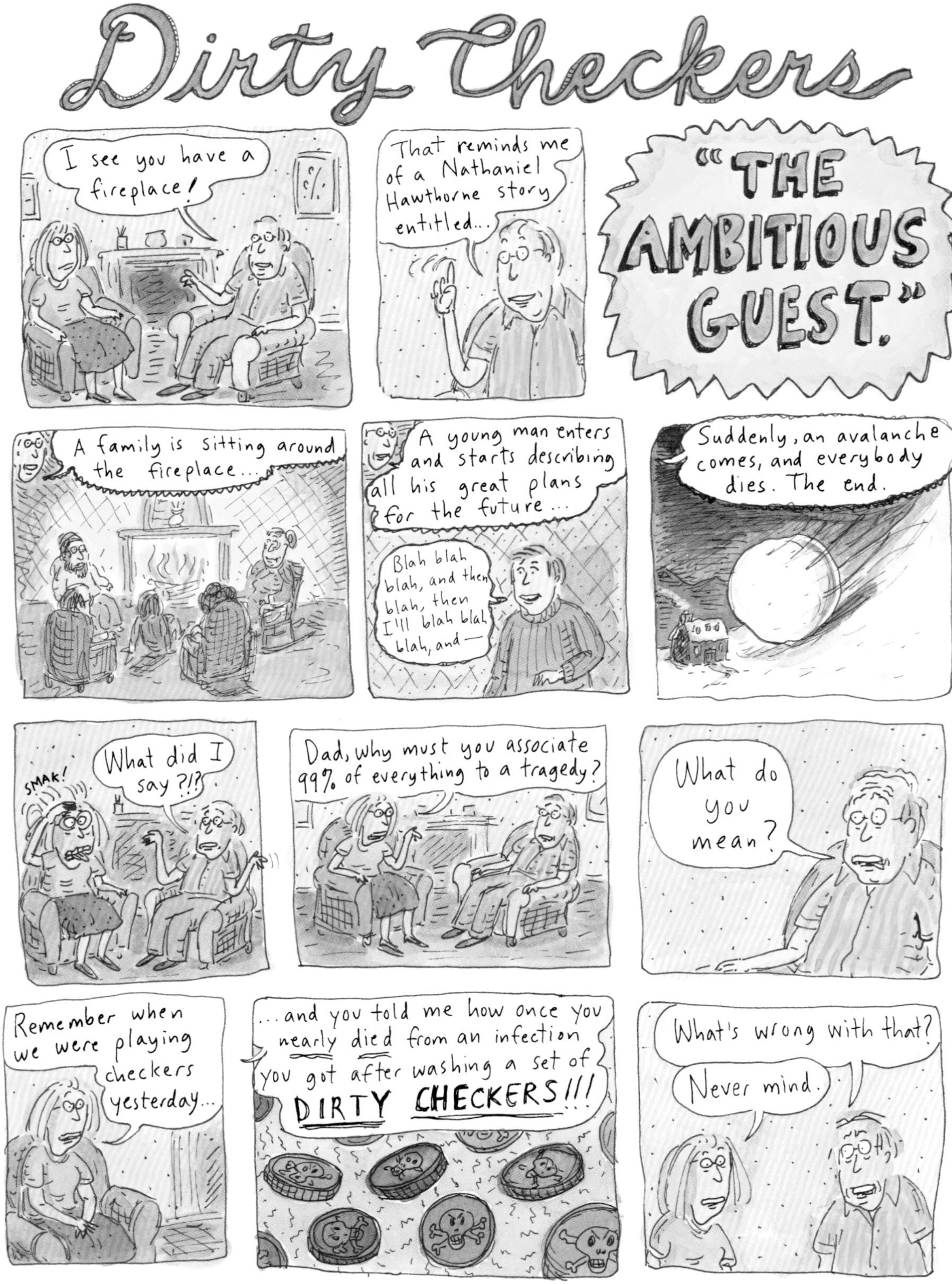
Dirty Checkers
I see you have a fireplace!
That reminds me of a Nathaniel Hawthorne story entitled...
"THE AMBITIOUS GUEST."
A family is sitting around the fireplace...
A young man enters and starts describing all his great plans for the future...
Blah blah blah, and then blah, then I'll blah blah blah, and—
Suddenly, an avalanche comes, and everybody dies. The end.
SMAK!
What did I say?!?
Dad, why must you associate 99% of everything to a tragedy?
What do you mean?
Remember when we were playing checkers yesterday...
...and you told me how once you nearly died from an infection you got after washing a set of DIRTY CHECKERS!!!
What's wrong with that?
Never mind.

My mother was a different story. She was a perfectionist who saw things in black and white. Where my father was tentative and gentle, she was critical and uncompromising.

She had once wanted to be a concert pianist, but she said, "It came too easily to me." She still played at home for an hour or so every night while my father and I would cower in admiration on the couch.

She had been an assistant principal in an elementary school for most of her working life, a job for which she was perfectly suited. She was good at telling people what to do. She was decisive, good in a crisis, and not afraid of making enemies. Those stupid enough to get her angry got what she liked to call "a blast from Chast."

My father and I were often on the receiving end of these "blasts from Chast," in spite of our best efforts to avoid them. She was often angry with him for being slow or messy or incompetent, and with me for just being a kid and therefore generally annoying.

The words we both dreaded were:

I'M GOING TO BLOW MY TOP !!!

It implied not only a terrifying volcano-like explosion of rage, but also a possible stroke, something we both knew could happen because of her high blood pressure. And if it happened, it would be because we did it to her.

In fact when I was a teenager and saw the movie _Who's Afraid of Virginia Woolf?_, I thought: Edward Albee must know my parents.

A lot of my gripes have to do with generational differences. But some of it was personalities clashing. The two of them had their own thing going, and my being there complicated it in a way that did not bring out the best in any of us. I left for college when I was 16. I think we were all relieved. I could get out of the house, and they could go back to being just the two of them.

But now I was back. I didn't particularly like it, and they probably didn't either. Still, aside from running away from the whole situation and "letting the chips fall where they may," I didn't see a way out.

③

THE ELDER LAWYER

By October of 2005, they were both 93. They were getting frailer. There were a few more falls (my mother) and a few more incidents of forgetting to turn the burner off after making tea (my father).

They weren't leaving their apartment much. This was probably a good thing for other Brooklyn residents — I didn't like thinking about my mother driving, with or without an eye patch. I brought groceries to them. So did some concerned, wonderful neighbors.

A friend who had recently been taking care of her 90-something-year-old mother told me about Elder Lawyers, and I decided it was time to call one in.

Elder Lawyers specialize in the two things that my parents and I found it most difficult to discuss:

DEATH and MONEY.

Things like wills, estate planning, end-of-life directives... that kind of thing.

I knew that getting them to agree to meeting with one would be a hard sell.

Besides their aversion in general to talking about "unpleasant topics," there were also trust issues.

I'd heard about a dozen versions of this story over the years. Heartless children, elderly victim-parents. It was sad to think about them imagining me waiting in the wings and licking my chops. Plus, the whole thing was ridiculous: if I'd wanted a drawer of goddamn cashmere sweaters, I would have bought my own. I was financially independent— something I'm not sure they ever quite understood.

My parents had serious respect for money, the kind you have when you grow up without it.

A penny saved is a penny earned.

But once they had it, they didn't know what to do with it.

Put it in the bank...

The risky world of "high finance" was not for them.

...where it's SAFE!

They had always been renters, like their immigrant parents.

Too much responsibility, a house.

One big headache.

When my husband and I bought a house in Connecticut in 1990, they gave us some advice:

One thing: NEVER BORROW MONEY FROM A BANK.

They had no idea what houses actually cost in 1990. None.

Daddy and I can loan you $20,000 — even $30,000!!!

There were other things about moving out of "the city" they didn't understand.

So, how many TV channels do you get out there?

They understood: working a regular job where, when you retired, you got a pension; living in a building with a super; and putting money in a bank.

BROOKLYN BANK FOR SCRIMPING

Unfortunately, I barely knew anything more, which is why we needed to call in a professional.

THE ELDER LAWYER

Their careful scrimpings were scattered hither and yon.

He would have his work cut out for him.

I learned about their pensions. I learned about their taxes. I learned how much their rent was, and to whom it was paid. I learned about incredibly boring stuff like some account they opened up in 1979 where every month, they got a check for $53.17. We also did wills and filled out health-care proxy forms and power of attorney forms. It was all stuff I never wanted to know about, but that's what an Elder Lawyer was for: to help you learn about it.

He came to their apartment.

They allowed him to look at their financial stuff, which was a miracle.

BROOKLYN BANK for SCRIMPING

He even got them to discuss whether they wanted "extraordinary measures" to prolong their life in the event of, say, brain death. Talk about personal questions!

My mother's line about this had always been

I don't want to be a PULSATING PIECE OF PROTOPLASM!

But it's different when you have to sign an official document to that effect.

I do not want to be a pulsating piece of protoplasm.

I could see why it was weird. It's one thing to be 16 and say:

I'll never have plastic surgery! It's so phony and gross!

A person might feel different about plastic surgery when they're 50.

Everyone signed everything.

Elizabeth Chast
x
Greny Chos
x
Rosalil Clst
x

I got power of attorney. I did not buy a drawerful of cashmere sweaters.

GALAPAGOS

It was December, 2005.

One way to tell that you're still in Child Mode with your parents is when you want to impress them, even when you're thirty or forty or fifty years old. Maybe you just want them to be happy for you, or maybe you're looking to settle an old score. It could be both!

Maybe you got a promotion at work, or you got invited to the President of Earth's holiday party, or you won a Nobel Prize. Or maybe you want to tell your parents that you're going to the Galapagos Islands, a place they themselves had gone thirty years ago. And it's for **WORK**, which means: (A) you _have_ to go, and (B) it's even <u>cooler</u> than going there as a tourist, really. One must admit this fact.

I decided to bestow a call upon them, and let them "share the excitement."

✳ The "Crazy Closet" was what my mother called the large, deep closet in the middle of our apartment. It was our attic. It contained ancient coats and tattered bathrobes; an assortment of broken manual typewriters; a couple of those portable "record players" that folded up into a sort of suitcase; several dozen French and Spanish textbooks; a Styrofoam picnic hamper; an old Rexograph machine on which my father used to print French and Spanish tests in his teaching days; every single piece of luggage they had ever bought, all of it decrepit; blankets that hadn't been unfolded in forty years; and in the spaces left over, purses, ties, galoshes, fly swatters, board games from my childhood, and more clothes. They could not throw anything away.

There were aspects of their anti-acquisitiveness that I thought were admirable.

But sometimes they took it too far.

And a shopping trip with my mother could be somewhat surreal...

SHEER LUNACY

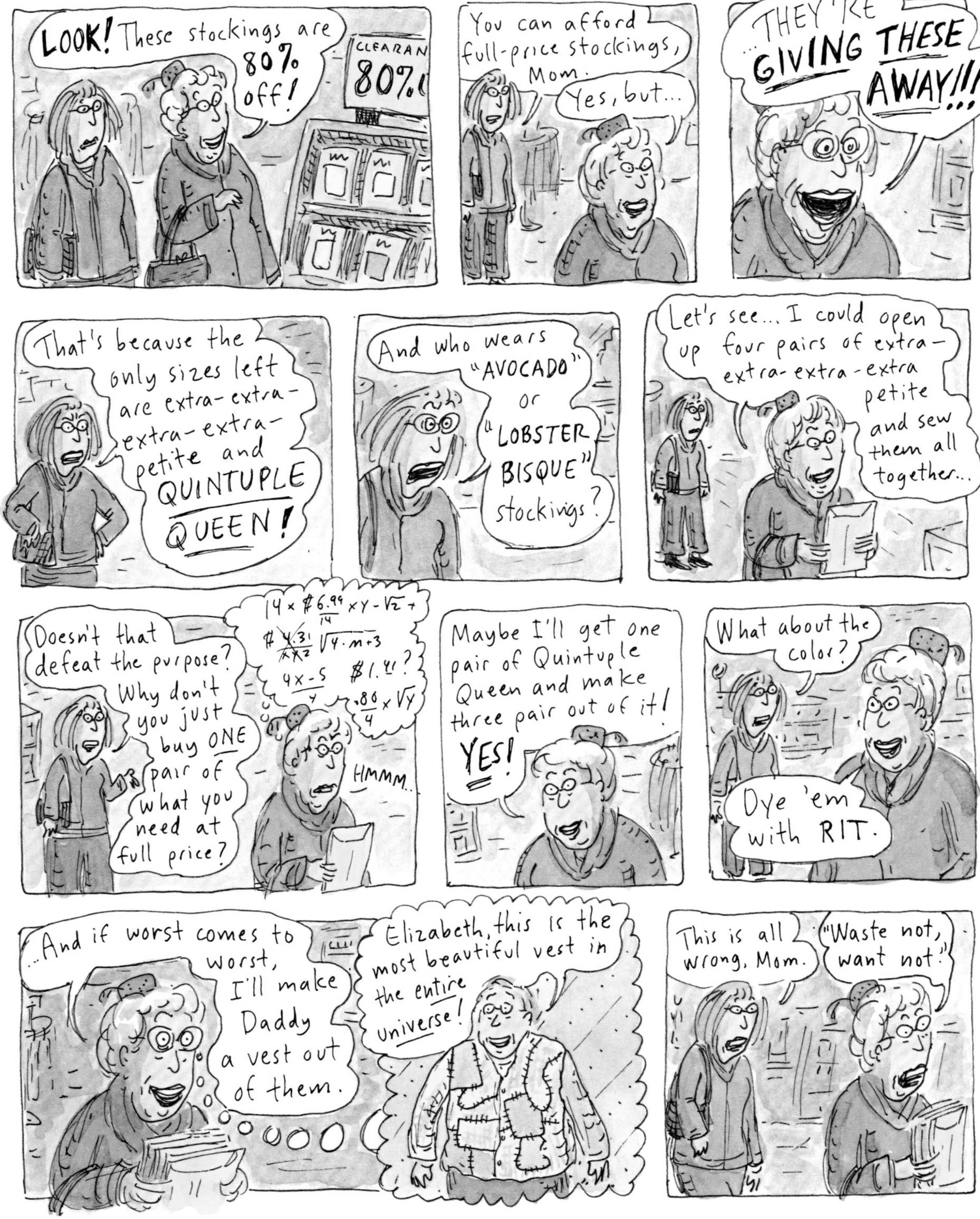

LOOK! These stockings are 80% off!
CLEARAN 80%
You can afford full-price stockings, Mom.
Yes, but...
...THEY'RE GIVING THESE AWAY!!!
That's because the only sizes left are extra-extra-extra-extra-petite and QUINTUPLE QUEEN!
And who wears "AVOCADO" or "LOBSTER BISQUE" stockings?
Let's see... I could open up four pairs of extra-extra-extra-extra petite and sew them all together...
Doesn't that defeat the purpose? Why don't you just buy ONE pair of what you need at full price?
HMMM..
Maybe I'll get one pair of Quintuple Queen and make three pair out of it! YES!
What about the color?
Dye 'em with RIT.
...And if worst comes to worst, I'll make Daddy a vest out of them.
Elizabeth, this is the most beautiful vest in the entire universe!
This is all wrong, Mom.
"Waste not, want not."

I was quite familiar with my parents' need to hold on to everything they had ever acquired. I also knew how compulsive my mother could be. I could sense that things were going in a direction I did not want them to go in.

A couple of days went by when we didn't speak. I had a bad feeling.

When my father answered the phone instead
of my mother, I knew immediately that the
news would not be good.

⑤

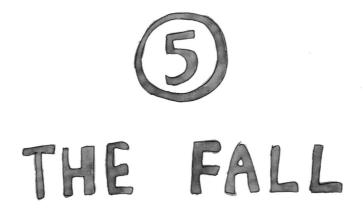

THE FALL

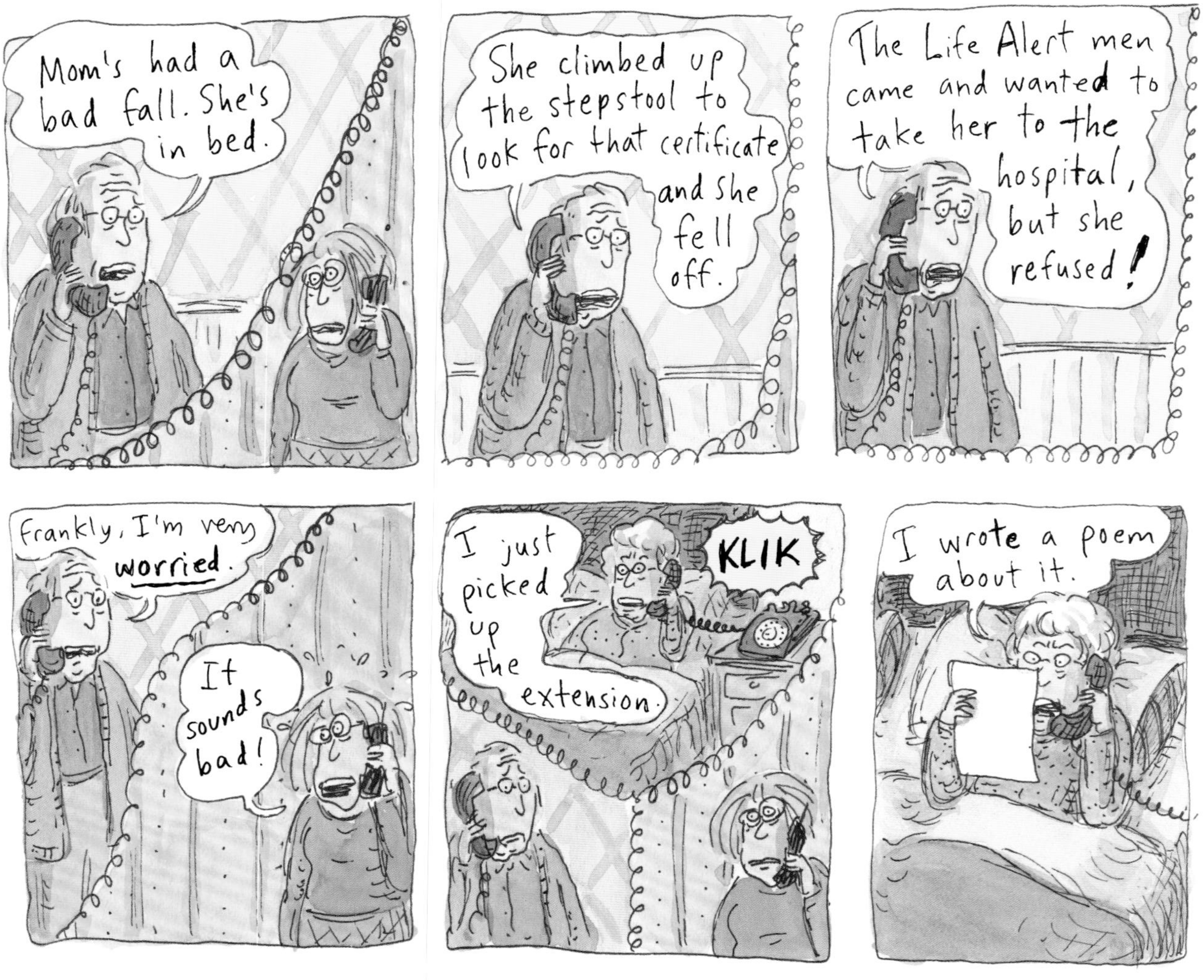
Mom's had a bad fall. She's in bed.
She climbed up the stepstool to look for that certificate
and she fell off.
The Life Alert men came and wanted to take her to the hospital,
but she refused!
Frankly, I'm very worried.
It sounds bad!
I just picked up the extension.
KLIK
I wrote a poem about it.

TOO SOON WE GROW OLD: TOO LATE WE GET SMART.

On the sixteenth of December
            Of two thousand and five,
I fell off the ladder,
            Bruised,----but alive.

I was mad at myself,
            I couldn't be madder
For being so dumb
            As to climb on that ladder.

At my advanced years,
            I am past ninety-three,
You'd expect more good sense
            From an old gal like me.

"Twas my knees that betrayed me,
            As they buckled under me.
This wasn't the first time,
            So just how dumb could I be?

So I fell over backwards,
            My head hit the floor
Nothing was broken,
            But my back is still sore.

ThANK GOD, I'm well padded,
            And I'm here to state,
I'm doing fine,
            For my age and weight.

Well, I'm not complaining,
            On the whole, I'm O.K.
But I'll surely be more careful
            Beginning with TODAY!

As I mentioned at the start,
            It's mankind's fate;
To grow old too soon,
            To get smart, too late!

ELIZABETH B. CHAST
DECEMBER 19, 2005.

My mother had a strong aversion to doctors and hospitals.
It didn't surprise me that she didn't want to call in the cavalry.

She was built a little like a fire hydrant. Short and SOLID. She was quite strong. (My father was more of the spindly type. One of her nicknames for him was "Skinnyshanks.")

But as the days passed, it became obvious she was not well. She was experiencing severe abdominal pain. She was not eating. She had a fever. The body was not healing itself. It didn't seem related to the fall. It was something else.

I wasn't sure what to do either. My mother was such a strong personality, and neither my father nor I could persuade her to do anything she didn't want to do, even in her weakened state.

For a couple of weeks, I'd bring groceries, visit (i.e., sit by my mother's bedside and comfort my father), and go home.

THINGS WERE GETTING WORSE.

My mother was sick, and my father was losing it.

My mother had been in bed since December 16th, the day of her fall. On January 4th, 2006, when I went into the bedroom, I could see that she was in pain, and that something would have to be done.

My mother finally agreed to an insane-sounding plan, but it was the only one that would get her out of her bed: I would hire a car to take my mother, my father, and me to New Jersey, which was where my mother's 80-something-year-old sister lived. Her sister was a retired nurse and ready for duty. (I had mixed feelings about some of her medical know-how. At our wedding, she told my husband that if we didn't have "marital relations" frequently enough, our babies would all be retarded.) In any case, after ten minutes, my mother changed her mind and decided to stay put.

I know what **you** want. I know what **Daddy** wants. I know what my **sister** wants. But **I** know what **I** want, and **I** want to STAY RIGHT WHERE I AM. IS THAT CLEAR?!?...

She was still the boss, and she could still deliver a blast from Chast.

I stayed a little longer, and then went home.

Later that night...

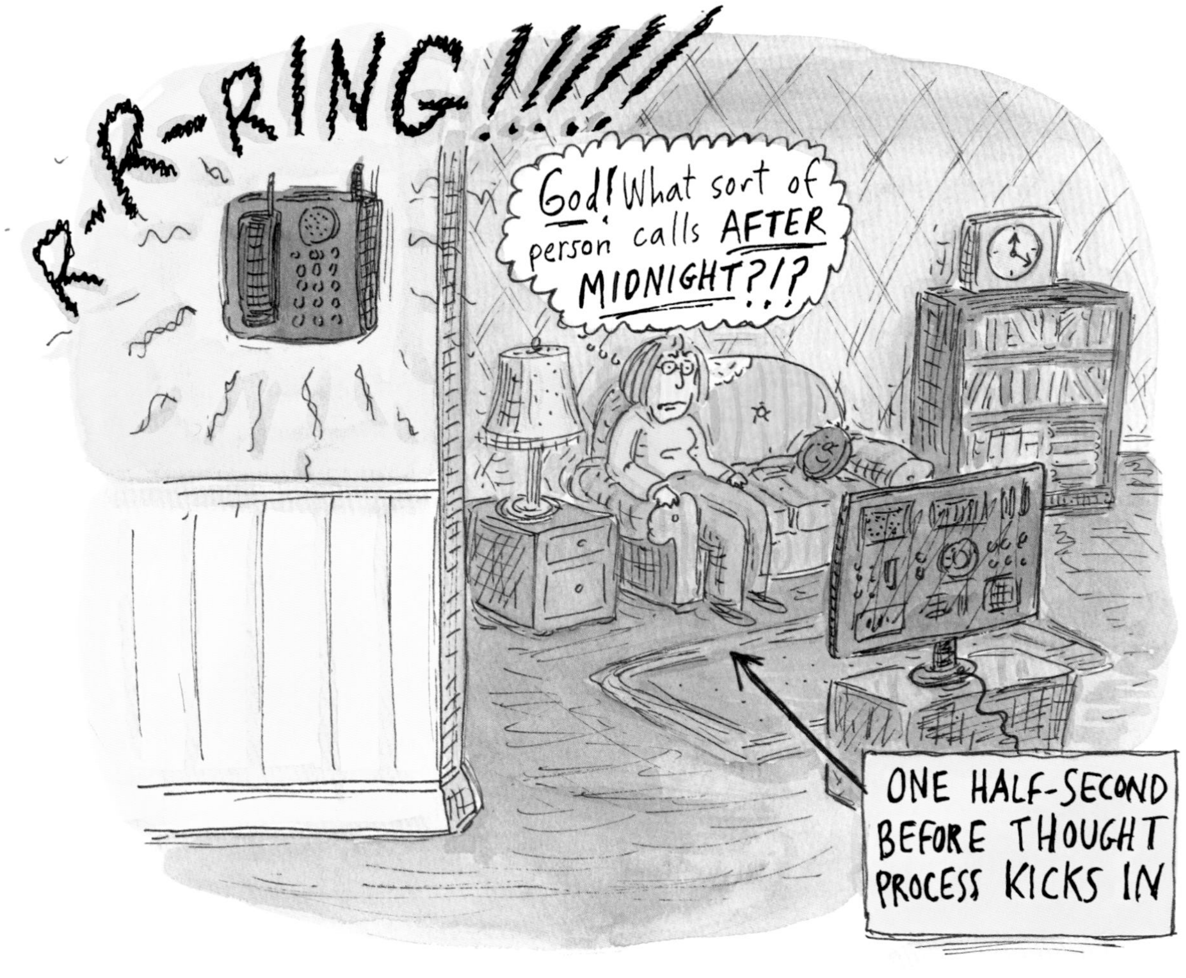
R-R-RING!!!!!
God! What sort of person calls AFTER MIDNIGHT?!?
ONE HALF-SECOND BEFORE THOUGHT PROCESS KICKS IN

It was a Life Alert sort of person. Duh. My mother and father were at the emergency room at Maimonides Hospital in Brooklyn. An ambulance had brought them both. My father couldn't be left alone, and he didn't know how to drive.

I didn't blame him for never learning. My own driving ability was limited. Anything outside of a 20-mile radius around my town caused a near-panic reaction. The thought of driving to Brooklyn, to a hospital (another fear), at NIGHT—forget it. I sat on the sofa for a few hours in an anxiety-coma. Finally, around sunrise, I got a car service to take me to Maimonides, and as I watched the world out the car window slipping by, wondered what would await me and whether I'd be up to the task of "dealing."

MAIMONIDES

I got to the emergency room at around 8 A.M. My parents had been there since around midnight. The E.R. was partitioned into little areas, separated by curtains for "privacy."

The hospital had run out of space in the E.R., so some people lay in beds in the hall.

HELP · HELP ME
HELP   HELP ME
HELP

My parents were in one of the areas. My mother was in a bed, and my father sat in a chair by her side.

There was a fair amount of moaning and screaming.

Time passed very slowly as we waited for a room to open up.

Tick...   ....
Tock...

Slowly, slowly, slowly...

Tickkkkkkk......

Had they *completely* forgotten about us ?!?

Tockkkkkk......

How I hated hospitals. The smells, the sounds...

Tiiiiickkkkkk......

Pain, illness, fear, dying, death... Morning turned into afternoon...

Tttoccccckkkkk......

Afternoon turned into evening... and then it was night... Perhaps we would be there forever.

Ttttttttttt......

My father looked like he might croak any second. We had been there forever. It was official: there was NO TIME.

PLINK!

At some point during the night, a nurse came in.

HEY!

62

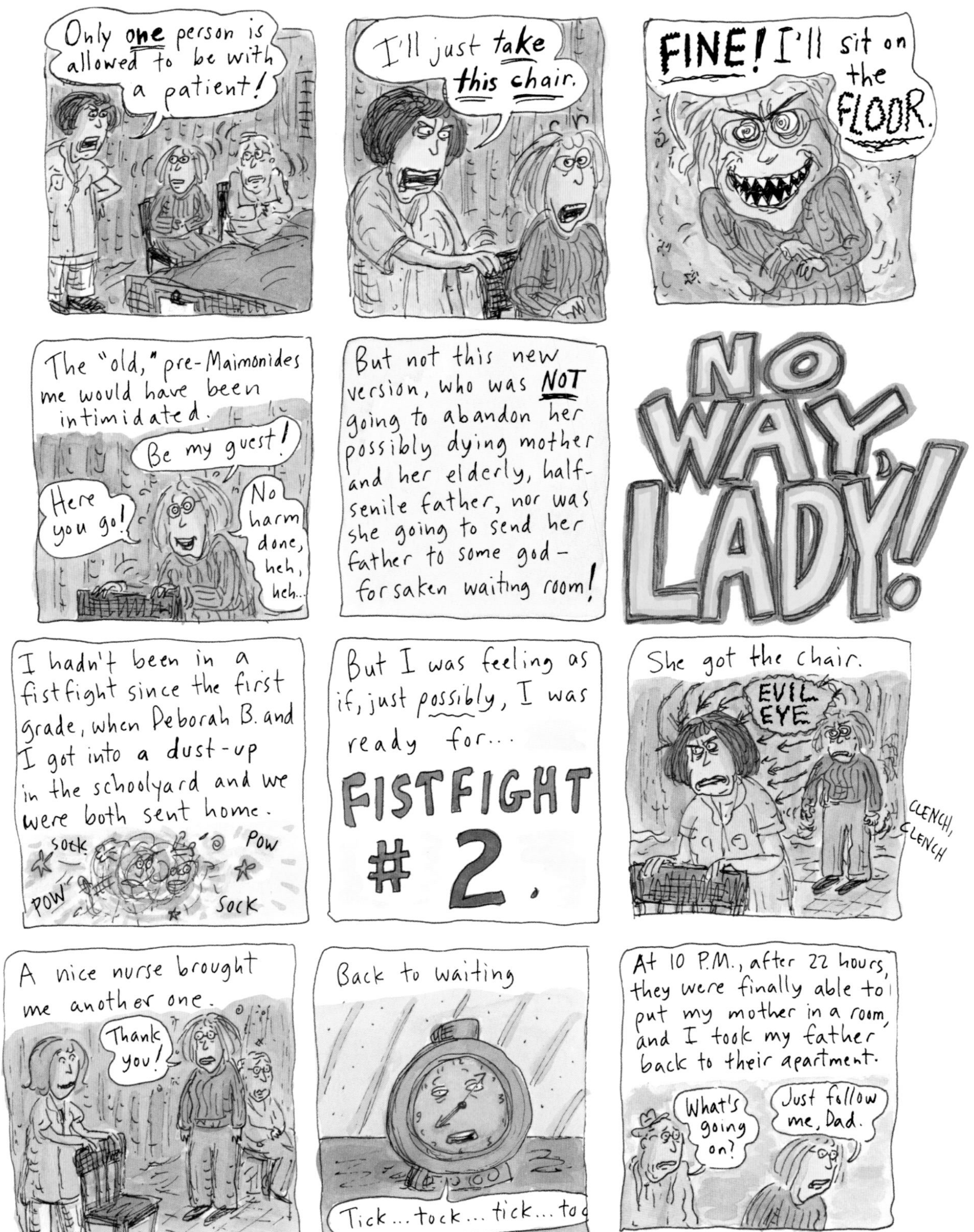
Only one person is allowed to be with a patient!
I'll just take this chair.
FINE! I'll sit on the FLOOR.
The "old," pre-Maimonides me would have been intimidated.
Be my guest!
Here you go!
No harm done, heh, heh...
But not this new version, who was NOT going to abandon her possibly dying mother and her elderly, half-senile father, nor was she going to send her father to some god-forsaken waiting room!
NO WAY, LADY!
I hadn't been in a fistfight since the first grade, when Deborah B. and I got into a dust-up in the schoolyard and we were both sent home.
SOCK
POW
POW
SOCK
But I was feeling as if, just possibly, I was ready for...
FISTFIGHT #2.
She got the chair.
EVIL EYE
CLENCH, CLENCH
A nice nurse brought me another one.
Thank you!
Back to waiting
Tick... tock... tick... toc
At 10 P.M., after 22 hours, they were finally able to put my mother in a room, and I took my father back to their apartment.
What's going on?
Just follow me, Dad.

I took my dad back to his home. He was extremely anxious, both for my mother's health and also at being separated from her. The only times they'd slept apart were during World War II and for a handful of previous hospital stays by one or the other.

We sat at the kitchen table and shared a beer. We were both exhausted. I tried to reassure him that everything would be o.k., and he went to bed. I pulled out the mattress in the sofa and went to bed too. It was very strange—it was the first time I'd slept in my parents' apartment since I was 22, when I graduated from college but hadn't moved into my own place.

The next morning:

I had had __no idea__ that my father was so far gone. When he was living with my take-charge mother in familiar, never-changing surroundings, his symptoms of senility had seemed pretty low-key. Certainly not this level of confusion.

One of the worst parts of senility must be that you have to get terrible news over and over again.

On the other hand, maybe in between the times of knowing the bad news, you get to forget it and live as if everything was hunky-dory.

Either way, there was no way I wanted to stay in that apartment. Plus, I couldn't – my kids were home in Connecticut.

I took my dad home – to _my_ house – with me.

When an unexpected illness struckdown the invincible

A random meteor
Shattered my world from above
Disrupting the lives
Of those whom I love

My husband my daughter
Are caught in the storm's wake (swirling)
But I shall overcome this
For all of ours sake —

Possibility of impact
Always was there
But we lead our lives
Not knowing when or where.

My routines, my compass
Went up in smoke
In flames and debris so thick
One could choke.

But we cant lead our lives
In fear of what might be
So live each day to its utmost
Only then will you be free.

E. B Chast Hospital, Bklyn.
Maimonides Hospital, Bklyn.
Jan 15 2006.

SUNDOWNING

My mother's diagnosis was acute diverticulitis. The doctors kept her in the hospital for two weeks. They gave her antibiotics, and morphine for the pain.

Meanwhile, my father lived with us. Any Florence Nightingale-type visions I ever had of myself - an unselfish, patient, sweet, caring child who happily tended to her parents in their old age - were destroyed within an hour or so.

My father's encroaching senility pushed me to my limit. He had become a real chatterbox, the king of the non sequitur.

The nonstop chitchat was annoying, but what really drove me over the edge was his paranoia about **THE BANKBOOKS.** *

In the morning, it wasn't too bad. There would be one or two bankbook-related queries, and then we'd "move on."

* The "bankbooks" were a collection of canceled and uncanceled bankbooks dating back to at least the 1960s. As I said, they never threw anything away. These were the same accounts that earned them all those blenders. Many of them were from banks that didn't even exist anymore.

But as the day went on, he became more and more frantic. Nursing homes call it "sundowning." He convinced himself that a certain neighbor—someone who had occasionally picked up groceries for them and who had shown nothing but concern— was going to break into their apartment and STEAL THEIR BANKBOOKS. He also decided that this person was a Nazi-in-hiding because of her slight German accent.

We visited my mother in the hospital every day, and every day, we stopped by the apartment to make sure the bankbooks were o.k.

By 5 o'clock, we'd be back at my house in Connecticut, and the sundowning would begin.

...safety of the bankbooks...

I'm concerned about Mrs. ———.

...break into the apartment...

How do you know they're still there?

Where are the bankbooks?

...the bankbooks...

...bank-books...

What if she gets in the apartment and takes the bankbooks?

...MARAUDERS...

I think we should go back to Brooklyn and get the bank-books. RIGHT NOW.

...bankbooks...

How do we know what she did during WW II?

Isn't it a temptation?

I feel the need to check the bankbooks.

Mrs.——— doesn't like Jews, deep down.

Instead of screaming at him, or unconsciousing him with a cast-iron pan, I made a sign:

When the bankbook talk started, I'd hold up the sign. If he didn't stop _on a dime_, I'd make the universal gesture for " my mouth is now zipped shut."

There were other anxieties, too. He slept with his tattered wallet under his pillow, and sometimes he rehid it, and it would get "lost." Never mind that all it contained was a few bills and a few photos. No driver's license, no credit cards: he'd never had any of those things. His beloved Channel 13 tote bag, which accompanied him everywhere (my mother referred to it as his "security blanket"), would get "lost" too. Everything would stop until these items were found.

He wasn't the only one who was getting stressed out.

It's really easy to be patient and sympathetic with **someone** when it's theoretical, or only for a little while. It's a lot harder to deal with someone's craziness when it's constant, and that person is your dad, the one who's supposed to be taking care of <u>YOU</u>.

Eventually, he would remember the events in the recent past, but three or four hours later, it was as if my explanation and lengthy reassurances that "things were going to be o.k.," etc. would be forgotten and we'd be back at square one.

He was "bad at" using the key, so it was my job to unlock the door when we stopped at the apartment. Like a lot of old locks, it was glitchy and needed coaxing.

Taking care of my father didn't bring out the best in me. There were a couple of funny things, though.

Or, on the same shopping trip:

Dinner was tough. I felt as if I was dealing with a child who had never been taught how to behave normally at a table. It wasn't so much rudeness as his idiosyncratic approach to food, which was lifelong and unrelated to senility.

I loathed watching him cut with a knife. He didn't plant the blade and saw back and forth while applying pressure. He sort of scraped away at whatever morsel he wanted to place in his mouth. It was not only ineffective, but somewhat disgusting.

When I was growing up, all the serving utensils would always end up on his plate, which drove my mother bats. His plate would look like this by the end of the meal:

One time my mother told him it looked "like a spiderweb," which made me laugh. No one else thought this was funny.

The worst thing he could say about a food was:

It could mean he'd never had it before, or he thought it was spoiled or going bad, or that he just didn't like it.

He was convinced that he had a sensitive digestive system, and that he could not digest tomatoes, onions, green peppers, anything spicy, or cucumbers. If we ordered pizza, on the very rare occasion, the slice on his plate would be decimated and dissected, and there would be a pile of paper napkins alongside it on which he had blotted off all the "extra oil."

Anything fried, "too sweet," or "too rich" sent him over the edge. It wasn't so much his not-eating these things as the little speeches that would accompany the not-eating, which seemed designed to make those who continued to eat those things feel like they were either hell-bent on self-destruction, or insensitive brutes with caveman stomachs.

If there was an apple pie in the house, it was impossible for him to cut himself a wedge like a normal person.

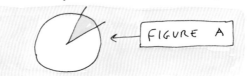

FIGURE A

He would slice off a big piece of mostly crust and then announce to anyone watching in amazement, "The crust is my favorite part!" never once thinking that crust might be other peoples' favorite part, too.

FIGURE B

His eating idiosyncracies – in fact, my parents' whole food dynamic – made me bats as a teenager. I just wanted them to be **normal**, or at least a little more like my friends' parents, who, as far as I could see, ate at normal eating speeds; cut meat in a conventional way; did not have a billion preferences and aversions; didn't have "favorite" cups and spoons and knives; drank beverages right from the refrigerator; etc., etc., etc. <u>Was that too much to ask?!?!?</u>

And now, here I was as an adult, dealing with this nonsense once more, and having to face the sorry fact that it still made me bats.

But mostly, it was just sad. Without my mother, he was lost, and outside of his familiar surroundings, he was disoriented in space and time.

Why am I here?

What happened to the apartment?

Tell me something: where do I live?

Where's Mom?

How long have I been here?

After two weeks, Maimonides Hospital decided my mother was stable enough to go home. Finally, they could be reunited.

THE END OF AN ERA

The night before my mother's release from the hospital, I brought my father back to the apartment. The alleged bankbook-stealing-Nazi-in-hiding neighbor volunteered to stay with him until I brought my mother home. It wasn't safe for him to be left alone, and luckily, he seemed to have forgotten his paranoias about the neighbor.

At the hospital, I dealt with all of the release-of-patient things, and arranged for an ambulette to bring us to the apartment. I had a pathetically large amount of pride in myself for doing things like that.

There was an insane amount of paperwork involved with her release, and that was only the beginning. Taking care of my parents meant that I had to collect and store a lot of information that I would be able to access readily.

I started keeping a notebook, just so all the facts and figures I needed would be in one place:

It contained my parents' social security numbers (required by practically every form I encountered); phone numbers of doctors, neighbors, relatives, the super in their building, various people I spoke with at their insurance agency; information from various elder care agencies — how much they cost, who came to my parents' apartment and when, and when I paid them; all the information related to their banking; anything about their landlord and/or lease; what medicines they took and what dosage; what forms were required by whom; all pension-related data; and much, much more.

Dealing with all of this "real-world," official, and essentially bureaucratic stuff combined two of my least-favorite feelings:

If you can pass the job on to someone else, I'd recommend it. If not, you have my total sympathy.

The ambulette men strapped her wheelchair to the bottom of the van so it wouldn't roll around. I sat with her and put her scarf on her head. We didn't talk much. At 8 P.M., we were finally back home.

My father was beside himself with joy and relief when she came in the door.

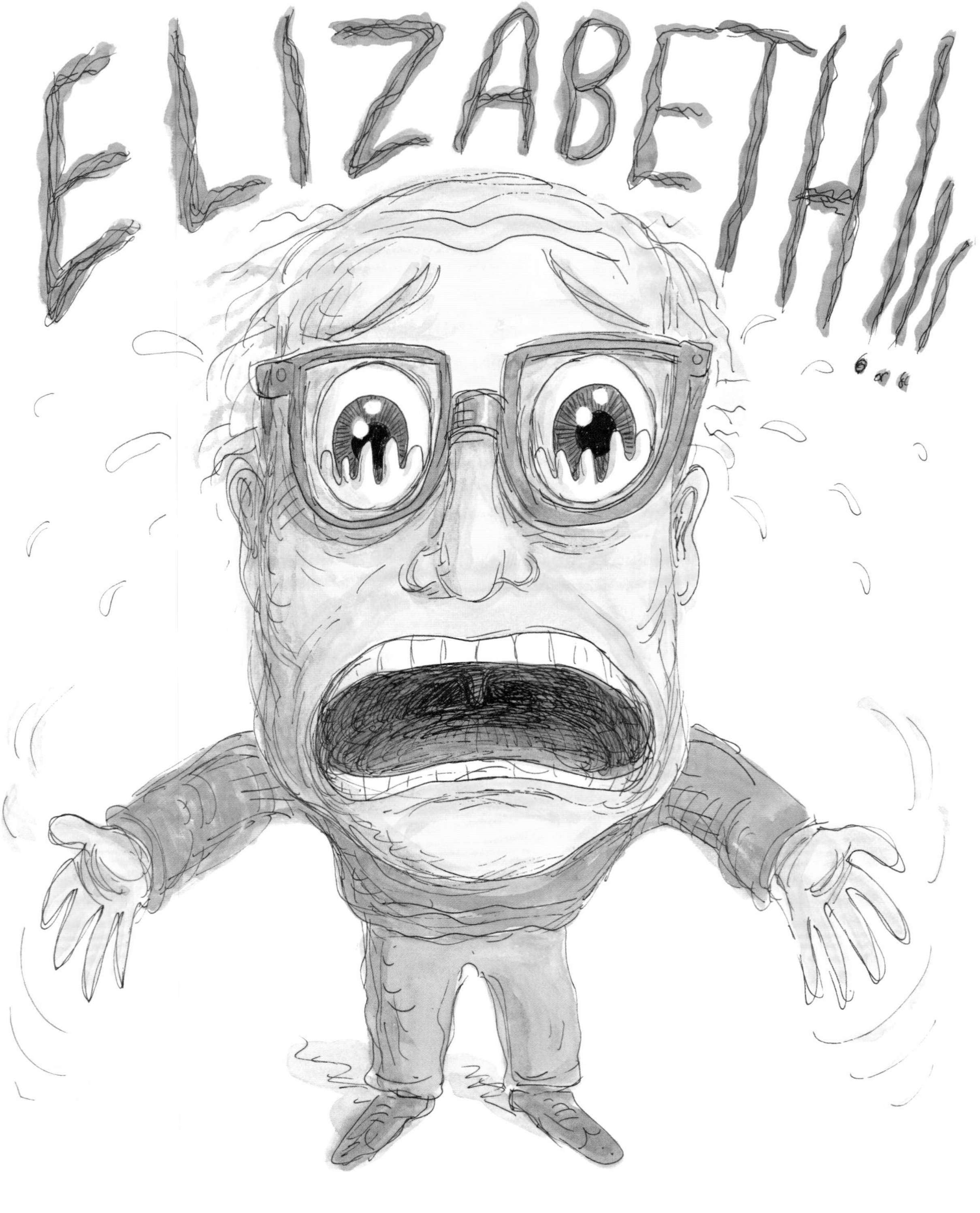
ELIZABETH!!!

There were lots of tears —mostly my father's. I stood there feeling a little "de trop," not for the first time in my life, and not for the last.

My mother was extremely weak. Two weeks lying in bed will do that. I got her into bed, got my dad settled, and went home.

How did I leave them like that? What could I _possibly_ have been thinking? Probably something like this:

I can't stay there! I **HATE** it there!

Besides, my family is back home in Connecticut! They need me _there!_

I'm sure they'll be fine.

Mom said I should leave, that they'd be o.k.

I have no choice. I have to go.

Why would she lie?

The next morning, I called to find out how things were going.

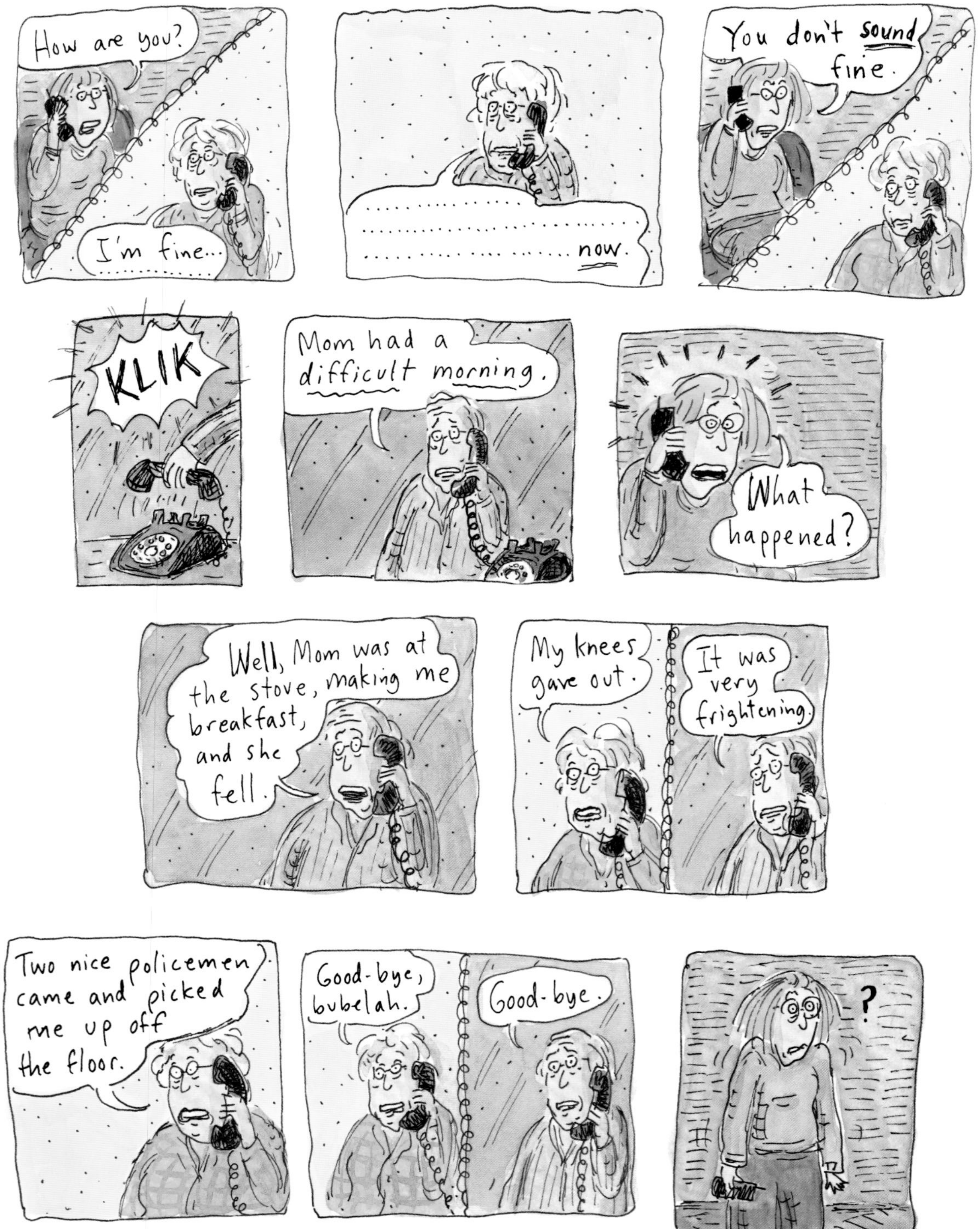
How are you?
I'm fine...
....now.
You don't sound fine.
KLIK
Mom had a difficult morning.
What happened?
Well, Mom was at the stove, making me breakfast, and she fell.
My knees gave out.
It was very frightening.
Two nice policemen came and picked me up off the floor.
Good-bye, bubelah.
Good-bye.
?

On the one hand, I couldn't believe she was at the stove, making him breakfast. On the other hand, it was ever thus:

THE MORNING AFTER

A PLAY IN SIX LINES

In bedroom. Elizabeth, who has just been released after two weeks in the hospital, and George, her husband of 67 years, are waking up.

Elizabeth: *(exhausted)* I'll make your breakfast now.

George: *(anxiously concerned)* Don't get up! I can get my own breakfast.

Elizabeth: *(impatient, testy)* Don't argue with me, George.

George: *(whining)* What are you trying to prove?

Elizabeth: *(enraged)* YOU'RE MAKING ME ANGRY! I'M FIXING YOUR BREAKFAST!! AND THAT'S FINAL!!!

George: *(resigned)* All right.

THE END

I tried to get them to accept even a little bit of help from outside.

We don't need any help!

They didn't want any strangers in the apartment.

We have many valuable things... like the bankbooks...

My mother insisted that no grocery store in Brooklyn delivered.

No, no. No.

No.

No, no, no, no.

No.

NO!

Occasionally, one of their neighbors helped out.

I'm going to the store. Can I pick anything up for you?

I continued to bring them food. But it really wasn't enough.

ICE CREAM

HAM

CHEESE

BREAD

SOCIAL TEA

MILK

They finally agreed to let Meals on Wheels deliver food. It was a godsend.

Mr. and Mrs. Chast! How are you doing today?

The food was pretty good, too.

Have some of the chicken. We can't eat it all.

But the grime and disorder were worse than ever, way beyond anything a mere "tidying up" could fix...

ANCIENT BOX OF SANITARY NAPKINS IN TOWEL CLOSET

KOTEX

And it was only getting worse. A friend of mine said:

You have found the source of the River Ebay.

ONE OF MY MOTHER'S LAST POEMS, ANNOTATED

Me.

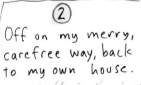

They weren't *that* brief.

THE VISIT

She[1] checked on her parents
And brightened their day.
But now her visit is over
She's off on her way.[2]

Her parents' lives are empty
No excitement, no change.
As days melt into each other
In a still ness so strange.[3]

They, who once travelled
All over the map,[4]
Are forced to lie down
For their afternoon nap.[5]

When the body demands it,
They must obey.
If they neglect it, they'll regret it
And rue it, the next day.

In their limited firmament,
Their heaven's brightest star,
Is their dearest daughter,
Their greatest joy, by far.[6]

Her visits, though brief[7]
Lengthen their days.
For her love and concern
Nourish her parents, always.

ELIZABETH B. CHAST
Brooklyn, N.Y. July 7th, 2006

Off on my merry, carefree way, back to my own house.

'Bye.

For pity's sake, stop

O.K., I get it.

TICK TOCK TOCK TICK TICK TICK TOCK TOCK TICK TICK TOCK

My mother "made" my father go on a final trip to Israel in 2005, when they were both 93, with a group of retired teachers. When they got back, my father remembered NOTHING.

They slept a lot that last year. That is a fact.

93

2006 continued to unspool. My father's dementia also continued to unspool. The phone calls from them were not comforting.

Your father won't stop talking! It's like a RUNAWAY TRAIN!

He follows me around the apartment! He hasn't bathed in months!

Yesterday he left the stove on!

My mother had never gotten back her strength after her diverticulitis attack and two-week hospital stay. She fell a few more times.

Mom won't use the Life Alert thing anymore, because she's afraid they'll make her go to the hospital.

Yesterday, she fell and a neighbor got her off the floor. I can't lift her!

Don't tell Mom I told you.

But anytime I mentioned "assisted living," the reaction was extremely negative.

Somehow, they were able to see through the euphemisms.

They stayed in their apartment for almost a year after my mother got back from the hospital. There were more falls, but nothing serious. She regained a little strength, but not enough to leave the apartment.

Food-wise, between Meals on Wheels, who delivered daily, a helpful neighbor or two who might pick up a quart of milk for them, and me, toting treat-filled bags from Grand Central Market every couple of weeks, they were o.k.

I had hired part-time help from an agency. A nice person — always female, often from the Caribbean — came to help out for a few hours three days a week. They did not particularly want anyone there. I think they only allowed it to get me off their backs.

It's an intrusion.

Besides, who knows who these people are? They could be anyone... We have VALUABLE PAPERS in the apartment!

I worried about them CONSTANTLY.

Then one morning my mother was getting dressed, somehow lost her balance, and fell.

My father couldn't pick her up, and because of the hospital fear, she wouldn't use the Life Alert pendant. He left their apartment to find a neighbor and somehow got lost in the building.

Finally someone retrieved him, brought him back to where he lived, and got my mother off the floor.

She was o.k., but at that point, even they had to admit that maybe it was time to make some changes.

THE MOVE

My mother decided that the three of us should check out a Place located in a distant part of Brooklyn where a friend of hers resided.

THEIR BUILDING

END-OF-THE-TRAIL FACILITY

We were there to "just take a look."

Stop panicking, George.

Except for an extremely difficult, life-shortening (for me) trip to the doctor's, my parents hadn't left their building for the past year.

I have...to...lie...down...

Elizabeth! Elizabeth!

I'll find a nurse.

I got them dressed, and slowly but surely, we went to see the Place.

Why are we doing this?

We're doing it for Rozzie.

Let's go.

By the time we got there, my mother was completely exhausted.

I...have to...lie...down...

I got a wheelchair and pushed my mother up to her friend's room...

...where she immediately passed out on the bed.

My mother looked very unwell. Her friend called for a nurse to come examine her. The nurse thought we should call an ambulance.

My mother roused herself.

No... hospital...

As soon as she had enough strength to get out of the bed, I called the car service and took them back home.

We didn't see much of the Place. What I saw was depressing: torn carpet; dirty, flaking walls; and lots of OLD, OLD, OLD, OLD people. Decrepit, hobbledy, sad old oldsters. Yep. →OLD.←

I got them back home. My mother was so weak she could barely manage the walk from the car, which dropped us in front of the building, through the lobby, to the elevator. The walk from the elevator down the hallway to their door was too much, so I guided her to the nearest stairwell, where she collapsed in exhaustion.

Meanwhile, my father was trying to open the door and having a meltdown. He was near tears and shouting about the lock being broken. I told my mother to sit tight (ha— as if she had a choice) and got the door unlocked. I got her into bed. The second I felt that it was even remotely possible for me to escape, I did.

Of all the stressful days I'd had with them since my mother's fall off the ladder, this one had been the worst, even worse than when she was hospitalized. At least then there were people around - doctors, nurses — who seemed to know what they were doing. Professionals in the land of the ailing.

Now I felt like it was just me, my mom, and my dad. And none of us had a clue.

Around this time, a distant cousin telephoned with an idea:

Maybe your parents would like to come to Missouri for a visit!

He knew their ages. He knew their precarious state. He and my mother spoke on the phone every few weeks. He was a DOCTOR, for God's sake !!!

I'll pick them up at the airport!

I knew he meant well, but he really didn't get it. For the extremely old, walking to the elevator at the end of the hallway is a real journey. They were no more capable of going through security, getting on and off an airplane, and dealing with baggage claim than going hang-gliding. HOW DID HE NOT KNOW THIS?!?!?

I thanked him, but declined on their behalf.

♪ Probably not the best course of action right now. ♫ But thanks! ♪

SOMETHING YOU SHOULD KNOW:

Once you pass your physical peak— let's say 25 - the falling-off is incremental. Every year—unless something "happens"— you get a little slower, a little saggier, until you hit 90.

At that point, things start to fall apart at a much faster rate. Which is why, when I hear about people trying to figure out how to live until they're 120, I want to ask them:

ARE YOU OUT OF YOUR MIND?

Less than a week later, I found a place about ten minutes from my house in Connecticut. It was important to take action. I had to move fast before they could change their minds. It was nice and clean and sickeningly expensive. But convenient. For me. And nice. And clean. They had an opening, too.

My parents agreed to come up for a "trial stay." They packed overnight bags, put on their coats and hats, and locked the door behind them.

It was February 23, 2007, and it was the last time they ever saw their apartment.

THE OLD APARTMENT

I was aggravated that they hadn't dealt with their accumulations, back when they had the ability to do so. That instead, when they decided to leave, they simply packed a couple of little bags and walked out, leaving me the task of cleaning out their apartment.

Still, I had to give them a certain amount of credit. My parents, who had never lived outside of New York City, at the age of 94, left their home of 48 years, along with everything in it, to move to a strange new home in Connecticut. And not just a regular home, but one that was specifically for old, old people. I'm sure they knew it would probably be the last place they ever lived.

Moving them to the Place was a huge relief, but there was a lot to be done once they were there. Everything involved paperwork and phone calls where you'd be on hold for twenty minutes and then hear an ominous click, followed by a dial tone.

They hadn't dealt with much of their mail in the last year. There was a gigantic pile of unopened envelopes, catalogues, junk mail, and Chinese take-out menus on the table when you walked into their apartment. There were a lot of banking, tax, and insurance things in there too, all of which needed to be sorted out.

I brought them some things from their apartment to make it homier, as well as some clothes. I had to buy some furniture and beds for them. Oh, well— it was their money... plus the TV and telephone service... It all felt very strange. Almost like helping your kid set up their first apartment.

I began the massive, deeply weird, and heartbreaking job of going through my parents' possessions: almost fifty years' worth, crammed into four rooms. If I wanted mementos, it was now or never.

I knew people who, as children, "explored" whenever their parents were out.

I found a stack of my dad's old Playboys!

I found my mom's college diary!

I was not one of those people.

Better not.

So this was my chance to rifle through all the drawers, all the closets: EVERYTHING.

CRAZY CLOSET

Who knew what amazing treasures, what long-buried, life-altering secrets I might unearth?!?!?!?

There was no buried treasure. No Hermès scarves, no Chanel purses. No first editions, no Braque etchings. No heirloom china. (My mother believed in plastic plates—they were lightweight and didn't break.) It was pretty much dusty old junk.

But it was our junk, and the thought of never seeing any of it again was troubling. So I took some photos.

My mother's glasses- all from
"before my time."

Stapler from my childhood
Guess it still worked.

Museum of old Schick shavers.

Random art supplies.

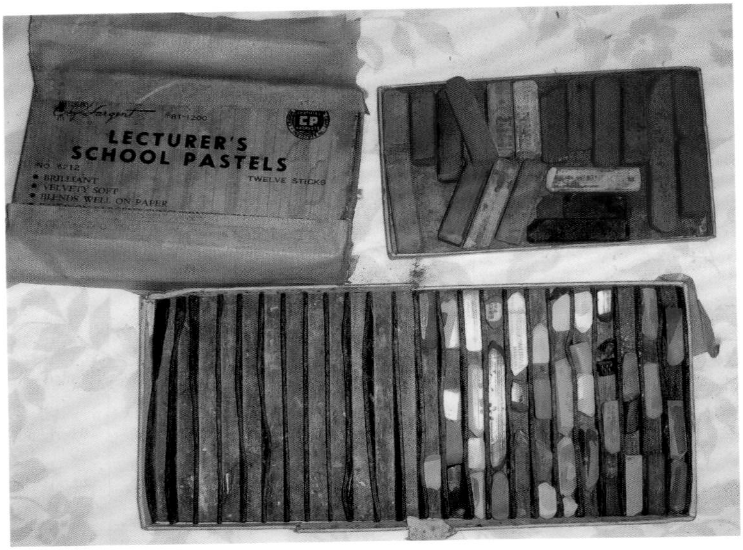
LECTURER'S
SCHOOL PASTELS
TWELVE STICKS
BRILLIANT
VELVETY SOFT
BLENDS WELL ON PAPER

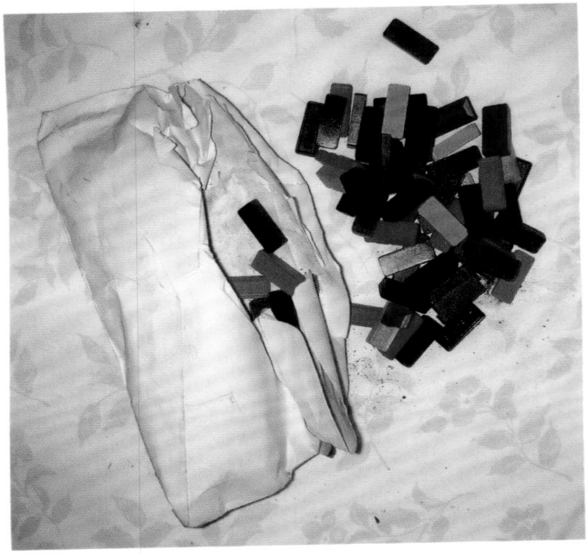

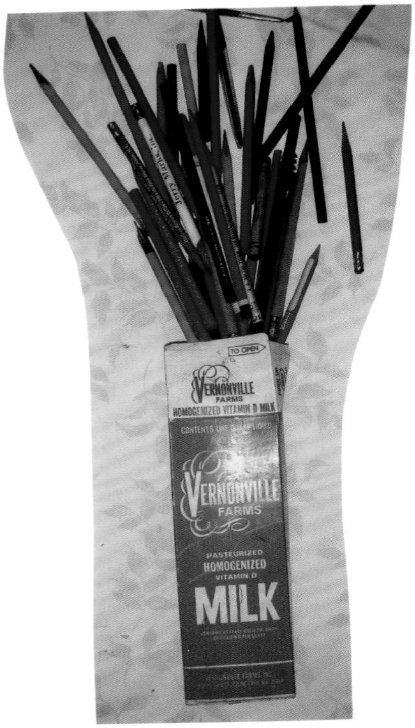
TO OPEN
VERNONVILLE
FARMS
HOMOGENIZED VITAMIN D MILK
VERNONVILLE
FARMS
PASTEURIZED
HOMOGENIZED
VITAMIN D
MILK

So-o-o-o-o many pencils !!!!!!

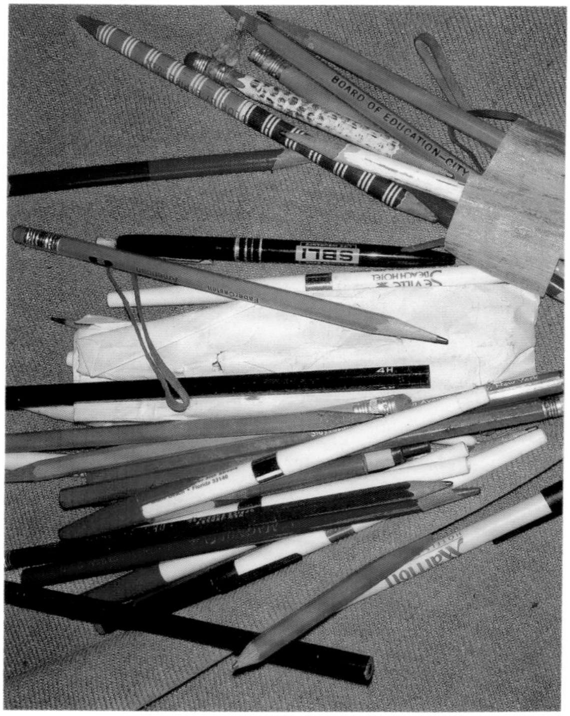
BOARD OF EDUCATION—CITY
4H

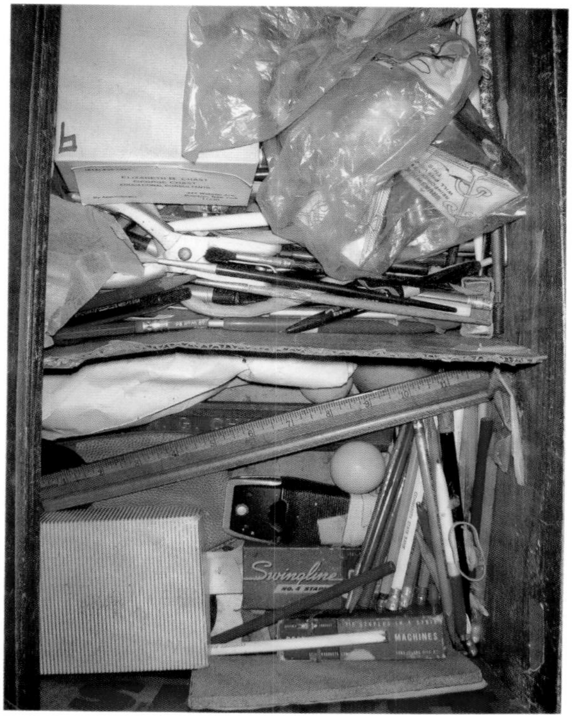
Swingline
MACHINES

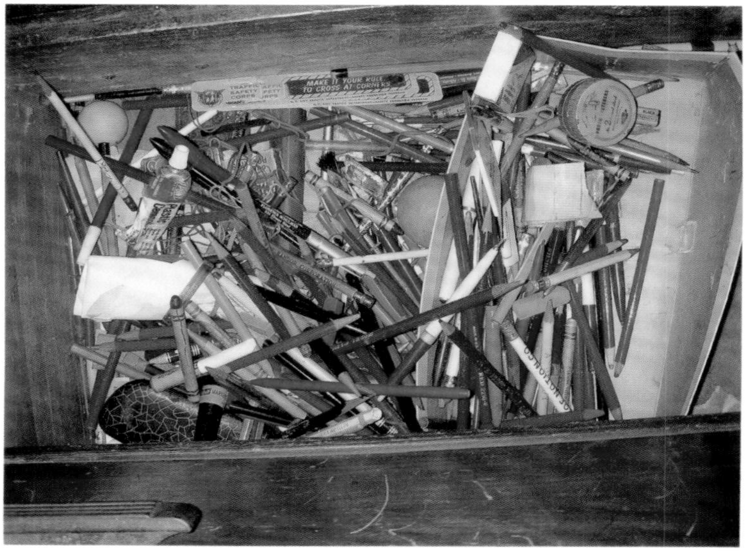
MAKE IT YOUR RULE
TO CROSS AT CORNERS

My parents' bedroom: how they left it.

I arranged all of my mother's purses on the bed.
In the background: ancient <u>Life</u> magazines.

This used to be my bedroom. Same horrible
linoleum of my childhood, same nice view of
the brick-walled side of a neighboring church.

One of my dad's "work stations."

My mother's "work station." Sign on left says:
"What is man? A mindless speck of confusion (floundering)
aimlessly (in a) meaningless void."

My old bed. Also, the filing cabinet - the
bankbooks were in the <u>back</u> <u>of</u> <u>the</u> <u>top</u> <u>drawer</u>!!!

In the kitchen. The blender is not "vintage style." It actually is from the 1950s. Close-up of photo in plastic thing: my eighth birthday party.

Why was there a drawer of jar lids?

Inside of refrigerator. The tins are from Meals on Wheels. The turquoise bin with all the tape on it is one of my mother's inventions and has been there since the mid-1960s. It's called "the cheese-tainer" and held-obviously-cheese. Don't know about the empty Styrofoam egg cartons.

Random shelf. My old baby shoes.

View of the Crazy Closet!

Inside of bathroom medicine cabinet.

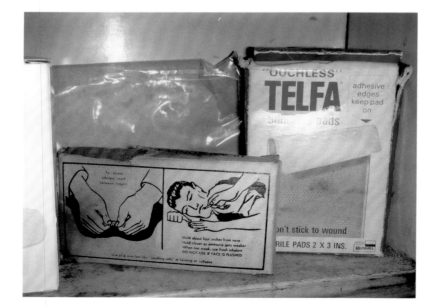

WHAT I RESCUED AND DECIDED TO KEEP:

Almost all the photo albums.

A pair of horse head bookends.

A bird picture I liked as a child.

Some silver pins I associated with my mother.

An evening bag of my mother's which I never saw her use. It was extremely out of character for her. Also, the tortoise-shell plastic lid had a crack in it.

CRACK

A small painting which disturbed but fascinated me when I was little. I didn't know what it was. Later, I realized it was an ocean at night.

A bracelet my father brought back from New Guinea, where he was stationed during WWII. Made from New Guinea coins.

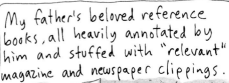

A book demonstrating embroidery stitches my mother made in some long-ago home-ec class.

FRENCH KNOTS   CHAIN STITCH

My father's beloved reference books, all heavily annotated by him and stuffed with "relevant" magazine and newspaper clippings.

BREWERS' DICTIONARY OF PHRASE & FABLE
THE Unabridged Dictionary
THE READERS' ENCYCLOPEDIA

A piece of Indian pottery my mother once told me was "valuable."

Miscellaneous photos; papers; a budget ledger from long ago; passports; and the bankbooks.

FLATBUSH SCRIMP   PENNY SAVER BANK   YE OLDE RELIABLE TRUST

The best find was three tattered, decomposing cardboard cartons tucked away on the top of a closet. One contained all the letters my parents wrote to each other from 1936, when they first met, and he lived in the Bronx and she lived in Brooklyn, until 1938, when they were married. The main topics were the weather and colds. One of them, or someone they knew, was always getting a cold, enduring a cold, or getting over a cold. As their "courtship," as my mother used to call this period, continued, the letters became more affectionate, but there was - I'm half sorry and half relieved to say - nothing racy.

The second carton held all the letters my father wrote to my mother during World War II, and there were literally hundreds and hundreds of them. He wrote every day, and sometimes he wrote twice a day. There were descriptions of Navy life: the accommodations, the food, the other guys. In 1945, he was sent to New Guinea, and the letters continued, with descriptions of the heat and mud and mosquitoes, and warnings not to go into the jungle because of headhunters and cannibals.

The third carton contained the hundreds and hundreds of letters my mother wrote back to my father during this same period, 1943 to 1945. They were self-described "cheerful little earfuls" about life back home: her work (she was teaching); her family; friends of theirs; her tonsillectomy; a strange party where guests took turns telling each other the thing they liked most about that person and then the thing they liked least. My mother disapproved.

And of course, their letters were filled with how much they missed each other, and how they looked forward to the end of the war when they would - "God willing" - be reunited.

I left everything else for the super to deal with. I didn't care whether he kept it, sold it, or threw it out the window. I was sick of the ransacking, the picking over and deciding, the dust, and the not particularly interesting trips down memory lane. I didn't want my 6th grade-graduation autograph book, my mother's piano, the console organ, any clothes, any linens, anything in the kitchen. I didn't want any of the falling-apart furniture that was ugly even when it was new. The knickknacks could all go to hell, along with my grade-school notebooks. I left thousands of books and records and manual typewriters and appliances and grimy liqueur glasses that were probably last used in 1963. Lamps and radios, galoshes, costume jewelry, good-bye. Is it possible there was something amazing hiding in the wreckage? Yes. Do I wish I had had unlimited time to comb through everything? Kind of. But where would I have put all the stuff? We have too much stuff as it is.

A friend of mine has an excellent rule when it comes to cleaning out your parents' house: if you don't think your kids are going to want it, don't take it.

It's no accident that most ads are pitched to people in their 20s and 30s.

I'm going to take up golf and tennis, so I'm going to need a lot of NEW STUFF!

Let's redecorate the house!

Not only are they so much cuter than their elders...

...but they are less likely to have gone through the transformative process of cleaning out their deceased parents' stuff.

Once you go through that, you can never look at YOUR stuff in the same way.

You start to look at your stuff a little... postmortemistically.

One day, my kids...

If you've lived more than two decades as an adult consumer, you probably have quite the accumulation, even if you're not a hoarder. SIGH

An ergonomic garlic press and throw pillows and those stupid sunflower dessert plates and seven travel alarm clocks and eight nail clippers and a colander and a flatiron and three old laptops and barbells and a set of FUCKING BOCCE BALLS, and patio furniture and an autoharp, for God's sake, and your old flute from high school and a zillion books and towels and sheets and a wok you never used and a make your own stained glass kit you never opened, and martini glasses and a yoga mat and what is THIS??? A cuckoo clock???? And so many clothes and hats and shoes and then there's all the KIDS' old stuff and don't forget the furniture and four cameras and ice skates and whose tap shoes are these? and all the crap in the drawers and...

THAT'S JUST THE TIP OF THE ICEBERG. I'm not saying I never buy stuff, because I absolutely do.

I must own this DEAR ORANGE SWEATER!

Maybe I'm less naive about the joys of accumulation.

Will this sweater bring me more than five minutes of joy?

Besides, I've got two just like it at home.

FEB 1966

Me at 11.

THE PLACE

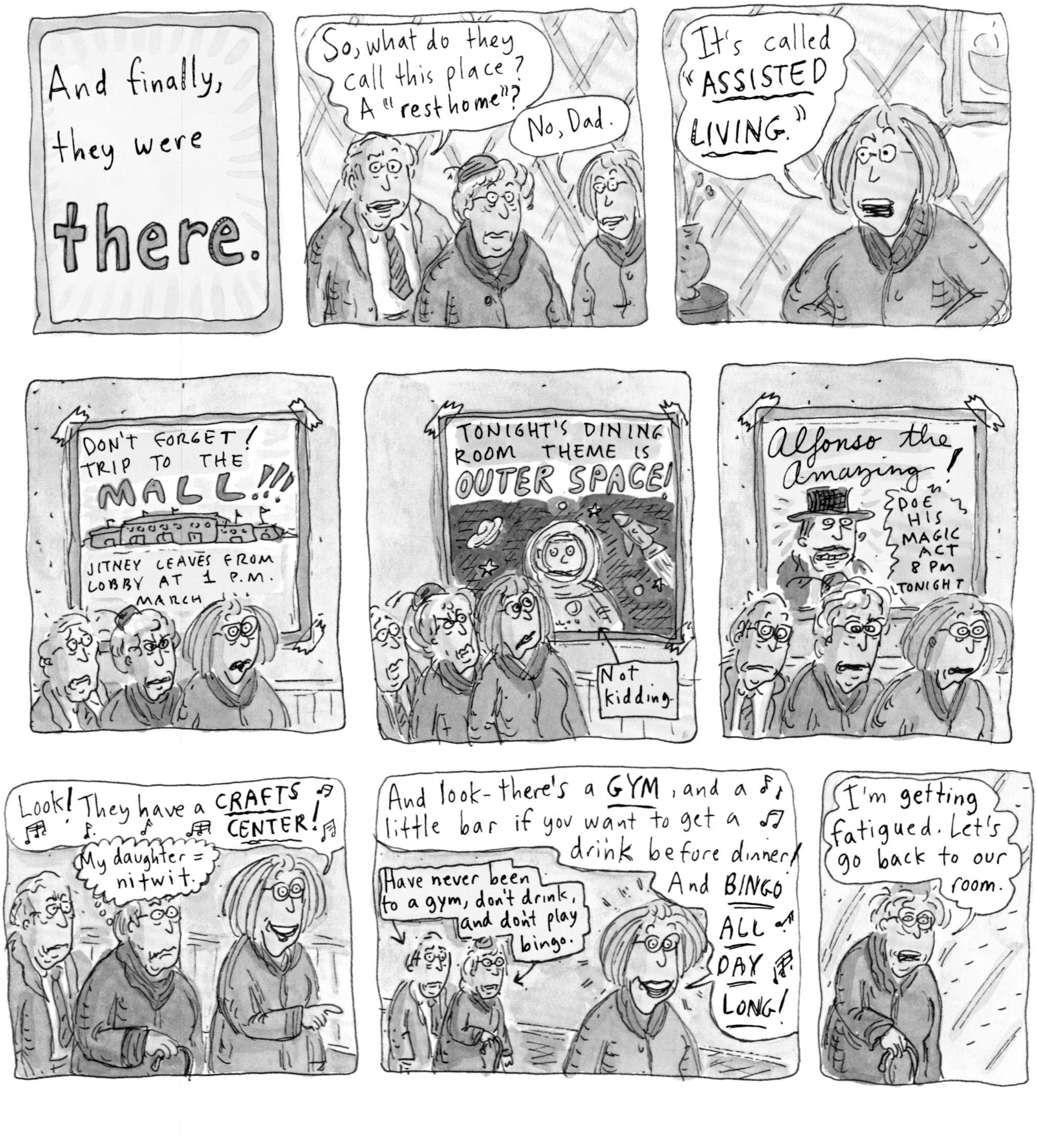

And finally, they were there.
So, what do they call this place? A "resthome"?
No, Dad.
It's called "ASSISTED LIVING."
DON'T FORGET! TRIP TO THE MALL!!!
JITNEY LEAVES FROM LOBBY AT 1 P.M.
MARCH
TONIGHT'S DINING ROOM THEME IS OUTER SPACE!
Not kidding.
Alfonso the Amazing!
"DOES" HIS MAGIC ACT 8 PM TONIGHT
Look! They have a CRAFTS CENTER!
My daughter = nitwit.
And look - there's a GYM, and a little bar if you want to get a drink before dinner!
And BINGO ALL DAY LONG!
Have never been to a gym, don't drink, and don't play bingo.
I'm getting fatigued. Let's go back to our room.

As Places went, it wasn't bad. It didn't make you want to kill yourself, like the Place in Brooklyn, which was dark and shabby and smelled like the end of the world. It was clean, and everything looked new. The decor could best be described as "Old-Person-Cheerful-Genteel." The main colors were nice pinks, safe peaches, inoffensive blues, soft greens, and harmless neutrals. The carpets and walls were patterned with unobtrusive stripes and tasteful flowers. There were lots of little decorative "touches": brass elephants, ceramic statuettes of people wearing costumes from some vague era in The Past, plants, vases, oversize bowls, sconces, etc. Muzak versions of songs from the '30s and '40s played quietly in the background everywhere. There were tons of seating areas, and a ledge at hand height lined all the corridor walls. A chessboard sat at the ready, but I never saw anyone play. A pool table gathered dust until bored teenagers visited. The jigsaw puzzle stations were quite popular, however.

127

My parents didn't have a clue about the Place's furniture or provisions policy. The rooms came unfurnished. The Place was happy to lend a few pieces (usually left by previous residents) until I could buy them furniture, for the additional monthly fee of $200, added to the $7,400 a month we were already paying. My parents had no idea what any of this cost. They never asked, and I never told them. And there were so many additional fees. The $7,400 included six hours of personal assistance from an aide per week, such as help showering or dressing. After that, you were moved to the "personal support plan," which added another $600 per month. None of this was covered by insurance. And furniture doesn't buy itself. Everything took time and cost money. It was enraging and depressing.

Eventually they settled into a routine. At the start, my mother was quite weak from the previous year of inactivity. She had hardly done much beyond walking from the bedroom to the living room and back. And that was on a **good** day.

One of the staff at the Place suggested I replace my mother's old, rickety cane with a walker, which was what many of the residents used. So I got her one - top of the line, of course. Not one of those Medicaid, aluminum-framed, lightweight, no-bells-or whistles cheapos for _my_ mother. At first, she was resistant.

Once you start using one of these, that's the end.

But it gave her more stability, and eventually she and my father were able to walk down to the dining room together to have meals and socialize with the other residents.

The Place served breakfast, lunch, and dinner, but the social scene really picked up at dinner. It was like the high school cafeteria, but with old people. There were cliques of people who had been at the Place for a while and who had bonded, and were not interested in anyone new joining them, especially ones who had the presumption to sit at their table without an invitation.

I'm sorry. These seats are all _reserved_.

You definitely didn't want to get stuck sitting with a Drooler or a soon-to-be Alzheimer's person, who was hanging onto her assisted-living status by her last fingertip, after which came the special Alz wing, with its own separate dining room. No one wanted to watch a person stuff his mouth with mashed potato but forget to swallow, so that eventually the potato mass would burst out of his mouth like an erupting volcano. Such sights were not only nauseating, but extremely depressing.

I got periodic reports on the dining room scene, mostly from my mother.

Sometimes one of their tablemates could be a little tactless:

But it was **true**. He **did** talk too much, and it wasn't all senility-related. My mother got critiqued too. It turned out not everybody agreed with my father that my mother was the world's leading authority about everything. Plus, I wasn't the only person who thought that sometimes she was too bossy. My mother loved to be right. But if you want to get along with people, you can't always be the Only Right Person in the World, or even in the Room.

They were out of practice with socializing. They had been each other's only mirrors for too long.

Afternoon at THE PLACE

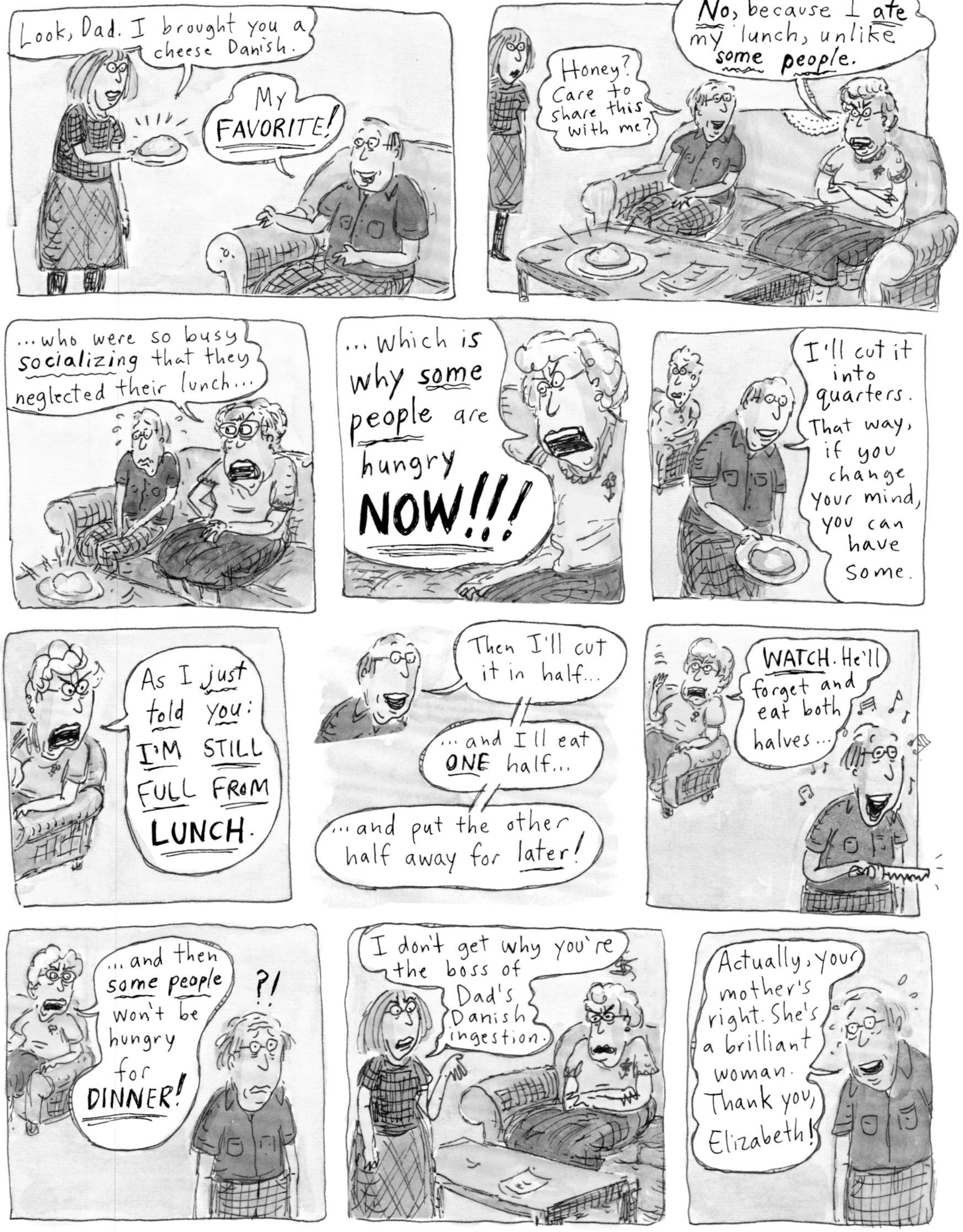

Look, Dad. I brought you a cheese Danish.
My FAVORITE!
Honey? Care to share this with me?
No, because I ate my lunch, unlike some people.
...who were so busy socializing that they neglected their lunch...
...which is why some people are hungry NOW!!!
I'll cut it into quarters. That way, if you change your mind, you can have some.
As I just told you: I'M STILL FULL FROM LUNCH.
Then I'll cut it in half...
...and I'll eat ONE half...
...and put the other half away for later!
WATCH. He'll forget and eat both halves...
...and then some people won't be hungry for DINNER!
?!
I don't get why you're the boss of Dad's Danish ingestion.
Actually, your mother's right. She's a brilliant woman. Thank you, Elizabeth!

I didn't feel **too** bad for them though. They had each other, which was a lot more than most of the people there.

THE NEXT STEP

The first few months were fairly uneventful, although sometimes I had the feeling that my dad was less than 100% enthused.

This place is a **HELLHOLE**.

I knew it wasn't a "hellhole." But even a top-of-the-middle-of-the-line, or bottom-of-the-top-of-the-line Place is still an institution, and institutions have rules.

Your father doesn't like to bathe.

AT THE WEEKLY ASSESSMENT MEETING WITH THE STAFF

My mother never called it a "hellhole," but she had opinions.

We're not "residents." We're inmates.

I'm sure it wasn't easy, but they were adjusting.

Your father had an egg in his pocket **all day** yesterday. Thank **GOD**, it turned out to be hard-boiled.

136

Sometimes I ate dinner with them in the dining room.

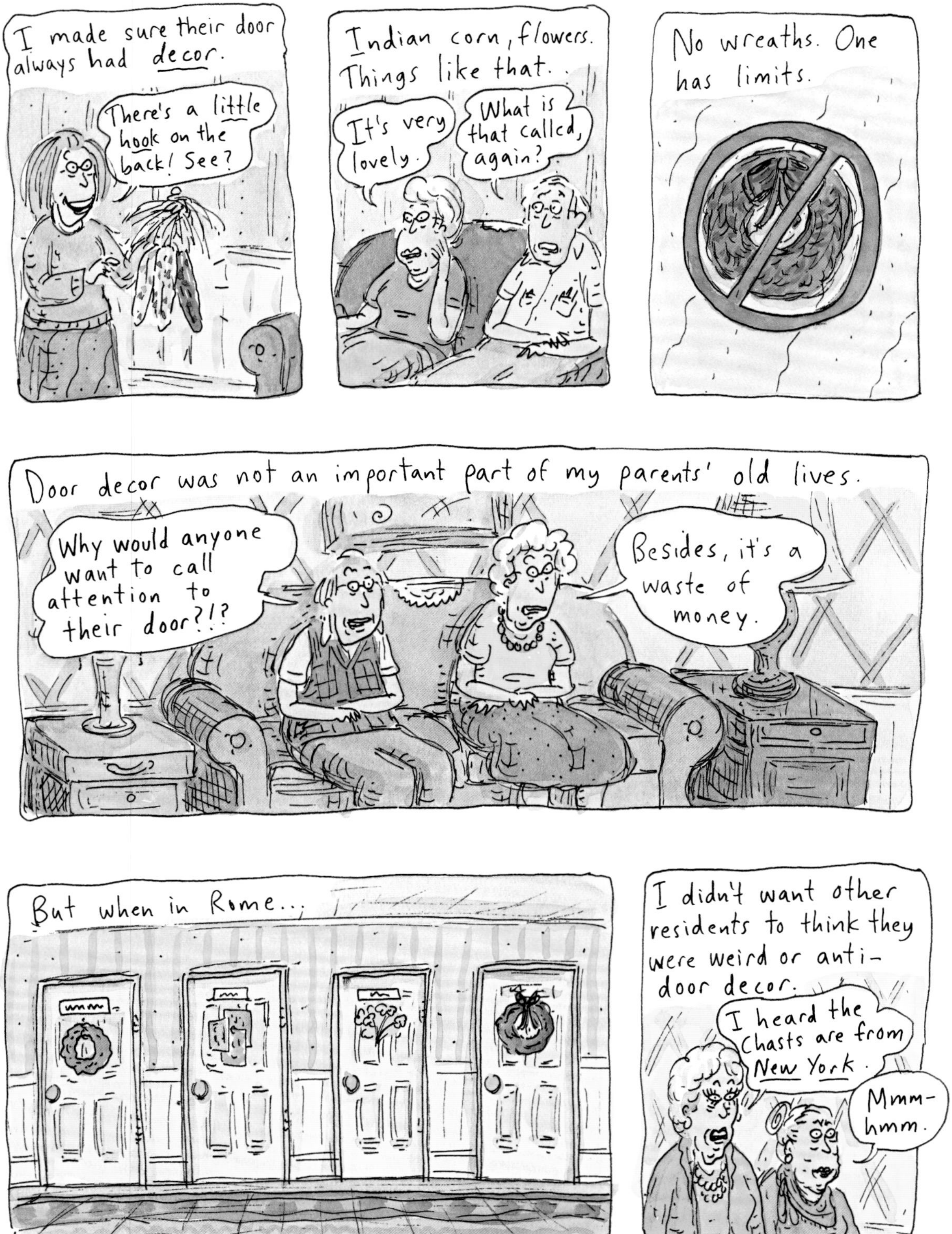
I made sure their door always had decor.
There's a little hook on the back! See?
Indian corn, flowers. Things like that.
It's very lovely.
What is that called, again?
No wreaths. One has limits.
Door decor was not an important part of my parents' old lives.
Why would anyone want to call attention to their door?!?
Besides, it's a waste of money.
But when in Rome...
I didn't want other residents to think they were weird or anti-door decor.
I heard the Chasts are from New York.
Mmm-hmm.

Then, one day in early June, about four months after they arrived at the Place...

It was someone from the Place, calling to say that my dad had fallen, and was going to be taken to the hospital.

What happens when people get very, very old is their bones get weak. Sometimes they don't fall and break something. Sometimes something breaks, and then they fall. In my father's case, it was a bone in his hip.

I drove to the Place. When I got there, he was lying on a gurney, awaiting transport to Danbury Hospital.

They fixed his hip, but after that, he was never the same. He refused to do any physical therapy. He was frail, alone, afraid, unable to toilet himself. He was 95 years old and TIRED.

I brought my mother from the Place to the hospital to visit him and back every day. I dreaded these excursions. I resented taking care of her. She never asked me anything about how I felt about my father's decline. It was, as it always was, completely about her.

My father was released from the hospital after a week, but his needs exceeded the level of care that "assisted living" could provide. He was put in a nursing home, just down the hill from The Place, where he'd stay until he was recovered enough to be reunited with my mother.

The nursing home was pretty depressing. There were no attempts to disguise what it was. No sofas, no sconces, no Oriental-style carpets. Just linoleum floors and institutional-color paint on the walls and hospital beds. There was a nurses' station in the middle of the floor, which was always surrounded by five or six very old, very out-of-it-looking people.

Once, I was walking by the station and a woman in one of the wheelchairs cried out to me, "Water! Please get me some water!" I went to get her some, but a nurse stopped me in the nick of time.

WAIT!!! DON'T GIVE HER THAT WATER! SHE'S JUST GOING TO THROW IT ON THE FLOOR!!!

He spent three weeks in the nursing home. He still
didn't want to do physical therapy, but he also didn't
want to change his position in bed. This caused terrible
bedsores on his hips and the backs of his heels. Nurses
would move him, but he'd move right back to where he
was before. He didn't want to eat. He was depressed and
disoriented. Worst of all, he missed my mother. She stayed
with him all day, but she went back to the Place at night.

Seeing my dad in the bed in the nursing home was painful. He
looked so small and so frail. How could this _be_? He was my
__DAD!__ But yes, he was "passing away." I could see it.

Finally, the nurses and doctors at the nursing home and at the Place concluded that even if he never really got much better, it was better for him in other ways to be with Elizabeth. It was decided that if I hired "extra help," via an outside agency, he could return to the Place.

For the first time, I was starting to have some serious financial concerns about all of this. Not just shock at the astronomical amount of money it was costing to keep my parents housed, fed, safe, and comfortable, and admittedly selfish bitterness about how much less there would be left for me when they died, but doubts about whether their money would hold out till the end.

I felt like a disgusting person, worrying about the money. But it was hard not to, especially when I thought about what this "extra care" might cost.

MINUSES: Rent, "personal support" plan, "concierge doctor" plan, rent for still-not-vacated Brooklyn apartment, cable, phone, laundry, community fee, furniture, medication, sundries... plus "extra care"... $15 per hour... 20 hours a week × 4 = $1,200 more per month.......

PLUSES: Mom's pension, Dad's pension... Social security... savings.

HOW MANY MORE YEARS???

My parents' health insurance plan, which they'd had since they began working in the New York City public school system, did not carry over into Connecticut, which was surprising and dismaying. They had "catastrophic" life insurance, which was useless as far as helping pay for assisted living, which was funny, because this sure seemed like a catastrophe to me. And they had Medicare — a bare-bones version, since they had never needed it when they lived in Brooklyn — which covered hospital stays and not much more.

GALLANT AND GOOFUS:
THE DAUGHTER-CARETAKER EDITION

Has forgiven her parents for all the transgressions of her youth, which she now knows were committed out of love.	Is still seething with resentment about crap that happened forty years ago.
Treasures the time spent with her parents, because she knows that soon, they'll be gone.	Mostly, when with her aged parents, wishes she were somewhere else.
Doesn't worry about the money, because if it runs out, she would be _thrilled_ to have them come live with her!	The idea of her parents living under her roof makes her want to lie down and take a very, very, very, very, very, very long nap.

KLEENEX ABOUNDING

Here's what I used to think happened at "the end":

One day, old Mrs. McGillicuddy felt unwell, and she took to her bed.

She stayed there for, oh, about three or four weeks, growing weaker day by day.

One night, she developed something called a "death rattle," and soon after that, she died. The end.

R.I.P. OLD MRS. McGILLICUDDY

What I was starting to understand was that the middle panel was a lot more painful, humiliating, long-lasting, complicated, and hideously expensive. My parents had been in pretty good health for their age - they did not have heart disease, diabetes, or cancer - but the reality was that at 95, their minds and bodies were falling apart.

Even with the extra care provided by aides from an outside-the-Place agency, my dad continued to deteriorate during that summer. There were no more trips to the dining room. He didn't leave the bed, and my mother didn't leave the room.

HOW TO PREPARE FOR VERY, VERY ADVANCED OLD AGE

Once or twice, I asked someone - a staff person at the Place, or later, a hospice person - what would happen when the money ran out. The response was always a variation of, "Don't worry! Somehow it always works out!"

At the end of July, my father told my mother that he wanted to "pack it in." He was tired of the work of staying alive and tired of his excrutiatingly painful bedsores. My mother did not care for his defeatist attitude.

I told Daddy he was coming with me to 100 if I had to drag him KICKING AND SCREAMING!

He entered hospice, which my mother didn't particularly approve of, either.

So, the hospice lady has started coming around.

She's very nice, but I told her: I don't want anyone coming around with a LONG, SAD FACE.

I want POSITIVE THINKING!!!

Not a bunch of people standing around singing "Kumbaya."

The "hospice ladies" did not always understand my parents' dynamic.

My mother was not comfortable with the idea of "palliative care." She saw it as throwing in the towel. But she must have known that he wasn't getting better and that the morphine was the only thing that kept him from screaming in pain.

His bedsores were very deep. His heels looked as if someone had taken a sanding belt and planed off the corners. I accompanied him several times on trips to the doctor to have them "debrided"— an ugly word for the ugly process of removing dead tissue. This process was extremely painful for him, even with the morphine.

Sometimes the morphine made him kind of "drifty." Once, on one of the debriding trips, he saw something on the floor but couldn't identify it. He asked me what it was, and I told him it was a Kleenex. He stared at it for a while — almost in wonder — and then suddenly said:

Kleenex abounding.

By the end of September, it was becoming clear, even to my mother, that things were not going to improve. The bedsores were not healing.

He developed pneumonia. On one of his trips to the hospital to have his bedsores cleaned, he was put on a gurney and taken to have his chest x-rayed. He looked so lost and sad when they wheeled him away. They found a "mass" in his chest. The doctors weren't sure what it was. Maybe it was an "enlarged heart." What did we think about surgery?

My mother and I did not think surgery was a sane or humane idea. If his bedsores weren't healing, what were the chances he would recover from major surgery? We didn't want to put my father through more pain.

He was given a DNR—Do Not Resuscitate—bracelet. My mother and I had to sign forms agreeing to this. She was hesitant, but I encouraged her to sign them, which she did. It means that the person wearing it will not be given cardiopulmonary resuscitation.

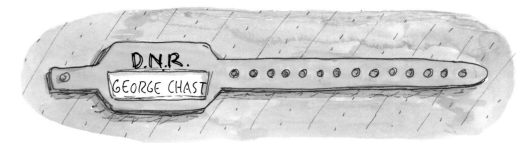

Around that time, I had a strange experience with a Ouija board.

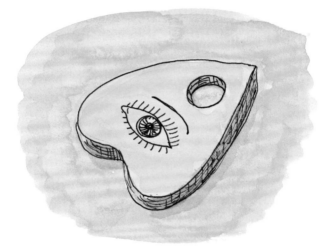

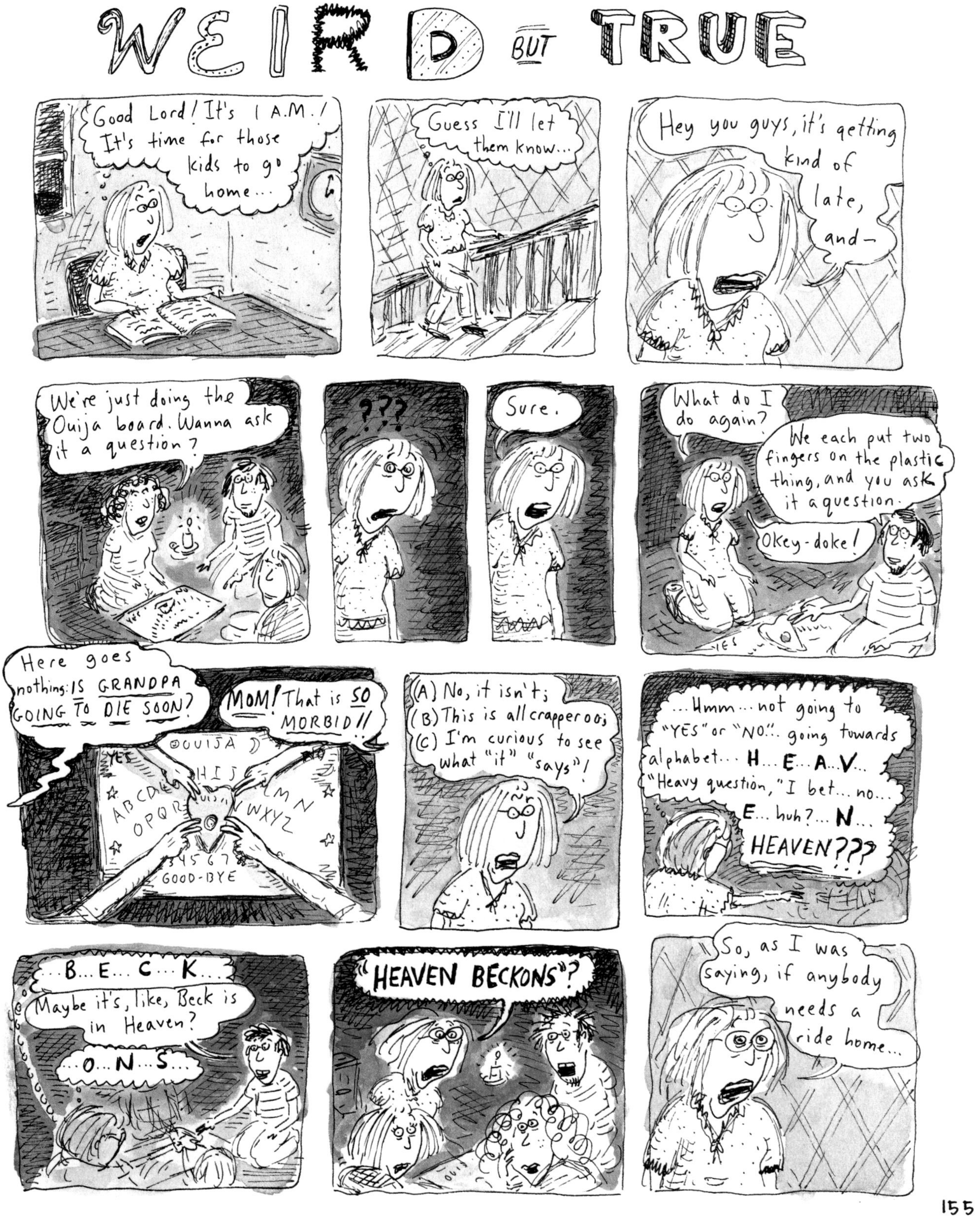
WEIRD BUT TRUE
Good Lord! It's 1 A.M.! It's time for those kids to go home...
Guess I'll let them know...
Hey you guys, it's getting kind of late, and—
We're just doing the Ouija board. Wanna ask it a question?
???
Sure.
What do I do again?
We each put two fingers on the plastic thing, and you ask it a question.
Okey-doke!
Here goes nothing: IS GRANDPA GOING TO DIE SOON?
MOM! That is SO MORBID!!
OUIJA
YES
NO
ABCDE HIJ
LMN
OPQR
WXYZ
3 4 5 6 7
GOOD-BYE
(A) No, it isn't; (B) This is all crapperoo; (C) I'm curious to see what "it" "says"!
...Umm... not going to "YES" or "NO"... going towards alphabet... H... E... A... V...
"Heavy question," I bet... no...
E... huh?... N...
HEAVEN???
...B... E... C... K...
Maybe it's, like, Beck is in Heaven?
...O... N... S...
"HEAVEN BECKONS"?
So, as I was saying, if anybody needs a ride home...

I don't know what it meant.

I don't believe in Ouija boards.

I don't believe in "Heaven."

I don't think any of us were moving it.

"Heaven beckons" is a weird phrase, not something any person in that room would use.

Anyway...

On the evening of October 16, 2007, one of my dad's nurses telephoned me.

Your dad is having difficulty swallowing.

She gave me a list of groceries to bring the next day.

- Boost
- ginger ale
- pudding
- anything easy to swallow

When I went to the store, I picked up some ice-cream sandwiches as well. They were his favorite.

The next morning, I went to the Place.

They had put my dad in the wheelchair.

I...I feel like I'm falling...

I tried to feed him some ice-cream sandwich

He seemed very, very tired. An aide and I moved him to the bed.

I curled up next to him and held his hand and patted his forehead. I tried to telepath to him how much I loved him, and that I knew how much he loved me, and that we were "good," and that it was o.k. to let go.

He said this to me:

What's Nina doing?

He adored my daughter, and she adored him. She had infinite reserves of patience for his endless, and endlessly repeated, stories about his father, the color-blind housepainter; how he liked to eat slowly and hated it when people like his brother-in-law rushed him; about word origins; about how much he loved the French language and how happy teaching made him ... she listened to him.

I said,

She's playing her banjo.

He smiled and fell asleep. It was our last conversation, but I didn't know that then.

157

I rejoined my mother, who was in a dither.

We have to call downstairs and get them to deliver lunch for DADDY!

WE HAVE TO GET HIM SOME SOUP!

There was some serious denial going on.

Mom, did it ever occur to you that Dad may be actively dying?

That did not go over well.

I DO NOT LIKE TO TALK ABOUT DEATH, AND I WILL NOT TALK ABOUT DEATH!!!

My father seemed comfortable. I was meeting a friend nearby for lunch.

I'll be back around three.

At around 2:15, my phone rang.

Your father is passing.

I knew it would happen soon, but not *that* soon

I drove back as fast as I could, but he had died ten minutes before I arrived. Joan, the hospice nurse, told me the sequence of events: that his breathing had deteriorated; that she and my mother were by his side; that at some point, my mother left the room for a minute to use the bathroom; and that's when he died. She told me that the phenomenon of a dying person choosing to die when his loved one left the room, if only for a moment, was one she had seen as a hospice nurse many times. She added that his death had been peaceful - that he just "slipped away."

I kissed his forehead, which was still slightly warm. It was so clear that he- my dad - was no longer there. He was gone, gone, gone.

Someone called the funeral home. They came to take the body away. Someone told me to sit with my mother elsewhere so she didn't have to witness the removal, so I did.

I brought my mother back to my house, so she wouldn't have to spend the first night without my dad alone.

GEORGE CHAST
March 23, 1912 – October 17, 2007

POSTMORTEM

It was a quiet drive. There was nothing to say. My father, who had been alive that morning, was now not alive.

I asked my mother what she wanted for dinner. She wanted pizza. I ordered pizza. Bill, my high-school-age daughter, my mother, and I sat around the kitchen counter and quietly ate some pizza. It felt surreal: I'm eating pizza. My father just died. Do you want another slice?

My mother looked tired, so I made up a bed for her in the living room, on the sofa. She couldn't walk up the stairs to the guest room. I told her I thought it was possible that someday, in some unforeseeable way, we would all be reunited. I didn't completely believe this, but I didn't completely disbelieve it, either. I tucked her in, turned off the light, and said good night.

The next morning, I got up early to drive my daughter to school. I noticed a terrible smell coming from the living room, but decided it was just a bad old-person smell. Before we left for school, my daughter wanted to use the downstairs bathroom, but the door was closed. I thought my mother might be using it, so I sent her upstairs.

When my mother didn't come out for a while, I knocked on the door and got no response. I felt a wave of anxiety and opened the door to find her slumped over on the toilet. At first I thought she was dead. Then I realized what had happened. My mother wasn't dead, but she probably wished she were.

My husband got my daughter out of there, and took her to school.

My mother had suffered one of the worst, if not _the_ worst, indignities of old age: loss of bowel control. The walls, the floors, the rugs were covered with excrement. Her clothing, her hands, and the sofa were caked with it. It was beyond imagining. I stood her on a towel (she was fully awake at this point, although in shock), removed her clothes, and washed her with warm, soapy water. Then I re-dressed her in some of my husband's clean clothes.

My poor, poor mother! Losing her lifelong mate of seven decades, then going through this awful humiliation. When she seemed to be a little less glassy-eyed, I drove her back to the Place.

We never spoke of what happened. Maybe there was really nothing to say. For a while, I thought perhaps she had blanked it out, but about a year later, she said to me, "I know why you don't have me over to your house. It's because you're afraid I'll shit it all up." So somewhere, she remembered. In any case, she was wrong: I didn't have her over because I _just_ _didn't_ _want_ _to_.

I wish that, at the end of life, when things were truly "done," there was something to look forward to. Something more pleasure-oriented. Perhaps opium, or heroin. So you became addicted. So what? All-you-can-eat ice cream parlors for the extremely aged. Big art picture books and music. Extreme palliative care, for when you've had it with everything else: the x-rays, the MRIs, the boring food, and the pills that don't do anything at all. Would that be so bad?

ELIZABETH, ALONE

My mother was very tough and very smart. I knew, because she had told me, that her I.Q. was higher than my dad's and mine: 152. Many people admired her, not just my father. She loved having authority, both at home and in the office of assistant principal. When I got in trouble in the seventh grade for drawing a caricature of an English teacher that I loathed, my mother came to my defense. But she was hard, and she had a temper. I gave up on ever trying to get "my way." I barely knew it existed.

Months before, she'd confessed something to me. I guess it was something she'd been wanting to get off her chest for a while:

I had blanked the experience out. But maybe that was partly why, for as far back as I could remember, I was afraid of her and her fearsome temper.

My feelings about her were complicated. That I knew.

After my father died, I noticed that all the
things that had driven me bats about him- his chronic
worrying, his incessant chitchat, his almost suspect
inability to deal with anything mechanical- now seemed
trivial. The only emotion that remained was one of deep
affection and gratitude that he was my dad.

This surprised me, partly because he had driven
me so bats in the last few years. I could still remember
all of that, but it didn't seem to matter.

My mother started to adjust to being widowed, and
I started to adjust to his being gone: to having just
her to deal with.

The first couple of months were tough. My mother blamed the hospice nurses for killing my father by giving him too much morphine. When I reminded her of the agony he'd been in from his bedsores, she said, "No, he wasn't." When I told her that sometimes I could hear him crying out in pain during telephone conversations, she said, "No, he didn't." My mother loved to argue, and she was good at coming up with alternative versions of events. She was so forceful, you could almost believe her.

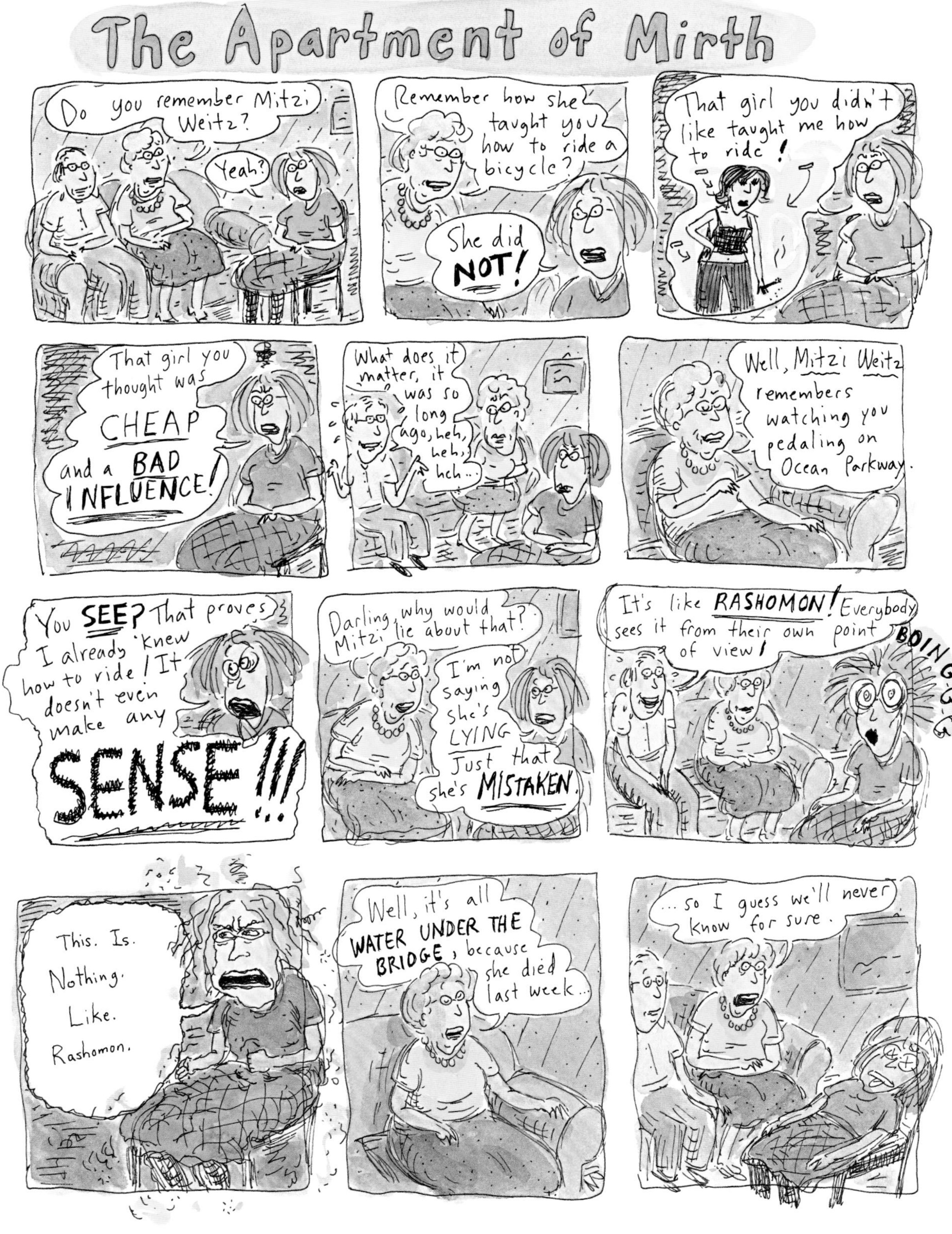
The Apartment of Mirth
Do you remember Mitzi Weitz?
Yeah?
Remember how she taught you how to ride a bicycle?
She did NOT!
That girl you didn't like taught me how to ride!
That girl you thought was CHEAP and a BAD INFLUENCE!
What does it matter, it was so long ago, heh, heh, heh...
Well, Mitzi Weitz remembers watching you pedaling on Ocean Parkway.
You SEE? That proves I already knew how to ride! It doesn't even make any SENSE!!!
Darling, why would Mitzi lie about that?
I'm not saying she's LYING Just that she's MISTAKEN.
It's like RASHOMON! Everybody sees it from their own point of view!
BOING-G-G
This. Is. Nothing. Like. Rashomon.
Well, it's all WATER UNDER THE BRIDGE, because she died last week...
...so I guess we'll never know for sure.

Getting my mother to leave her room and have dinner with the other residents in the dining room took some persuading, but eventually she decided it would be o.k. Sometimes I joined her there.

During that first year that followed my father's death, from the fall of 2007 to the fall of 2008, my mother's health declined slowly. But her chronic diverticulosis - the problem that had led to her hospitalization - was getting markedly worse.

I brought her to a gastroenterologist, who said she had a fistula in her lower digestive tract. He recommended a colostomy and said he was afraid she might die from sepsis without one.

On one hand, I thought: o.k., maybe he's right.
On the other, I thought: doesn't a colostomy involve surgery? And anesthesia? Wouldn't that be a little risky/painful/possibly insane for a 96-year-old woman for whom sitting upright in a chair for half an hour or walking fifteen feet from the sofa to the bathroom is a _major effort_?? And if she survives the operation, how does she manage the colostomy apparatus??? _HAVE WE ALL LOST OUR MARBLES_?????

My mother consulted with her sister, the retired R.N.:
You should have the operation! It's no big deal!

She consulted with me:

She decided not to have the operation.
No.

Around this time, my mother's health was steadily declining. She told me that she thought she was losing her mental acuity as well.

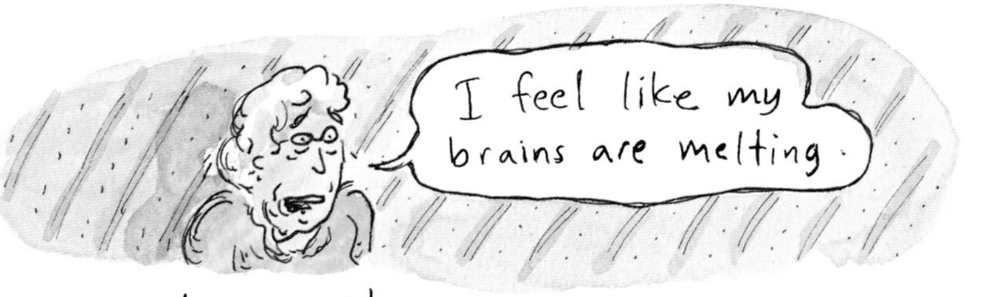
I feel like my brains are melting.

A neurologist paid a visit.

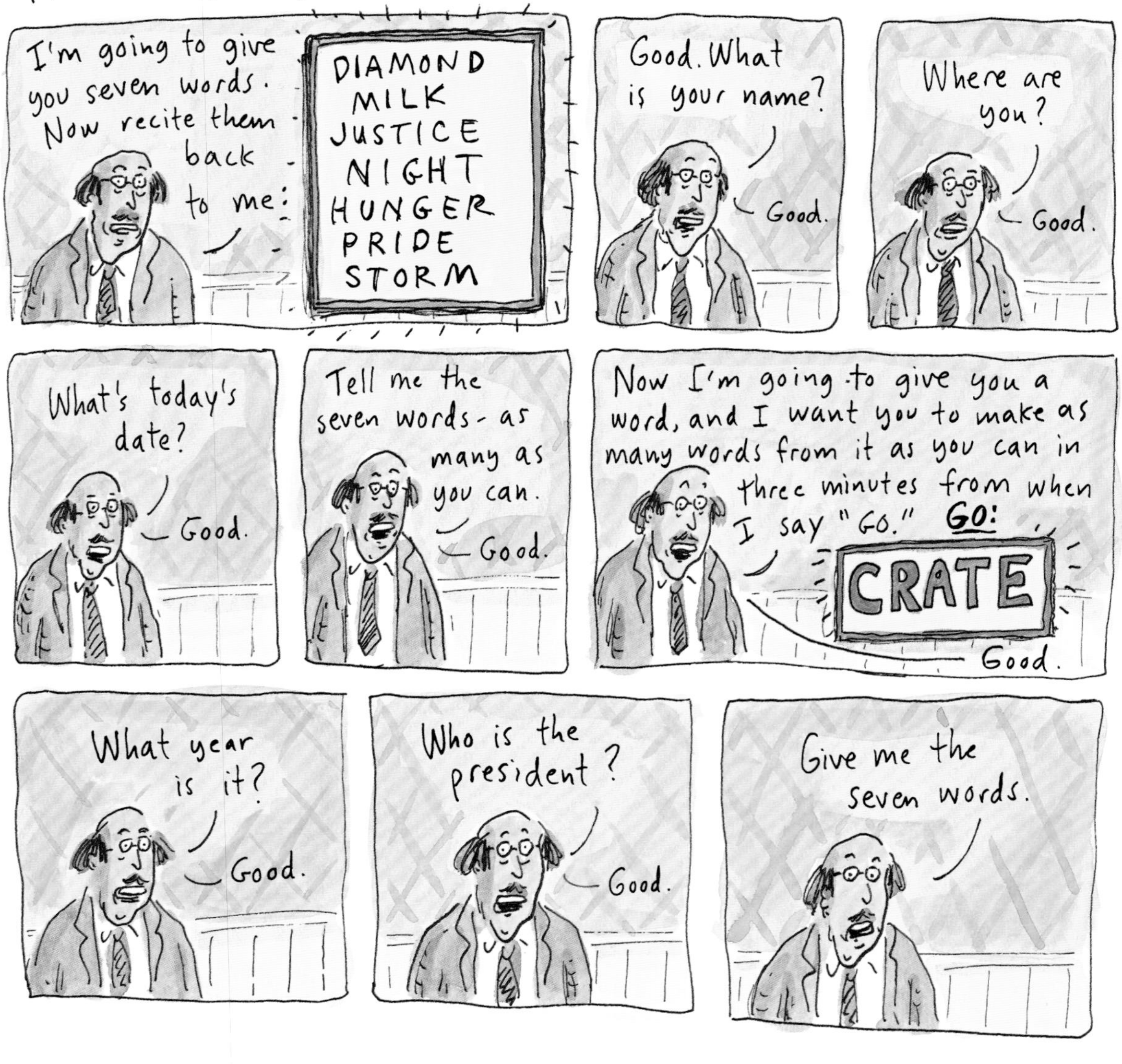
I'm going to give you seven words. Now recite them back to me:
DIAMOND
MILK
JUSTICE
NIGHT
HUNGER
PRIDE
STORM
Good. What is your name?
Good.
Where are you?
Good.
What's today's date?
Good.
Tell me the seven words - as many as you can.
Good.
Now I'm going to give you a word, and I want you to make as many words from it as you can in three minutes from when I say "GO." GO:
CRATE
Good.
What year is it?
Good.
Who is the president?
Good.
Give me the seven words.

The neurologist said my mother was depressed. He prescribed Lexapro. Her insurance didn't cover it — the only insurance she had was Medicare, since the plan she'd been paying into for seventy or so years didn't cross over from New York to Connecticut. Oh, well, no matter. That's what her diminishing savings were for.

By November 2008, she stopped going to the dining room. In fact, she had pretty much stopped eating.

She fell several times on her frequent nighttime trips to the bathroom. She refused to wear Depends or use a commode, which could be placed closer to her bed. Once she cracked a rib.

She lost fifteen pounds within a couple of months. Luckily, she was, as she often said, "built like a peasant." Sturdy. The staff recommended I get a hospital bed with sides that could be raised or lowered, which I did.

Her doctor started hospice care. She slept a lot. It seemed as if finally, she was giving up. I sat with her and said my good-byes and told her I loved her and that it was "o.k. to let go," a phrase I learned from the hospice people.

O.K. TO LET GO
THE WORK OF DYING
PALLIATIVE CARE

173

The Place suggested that I get around-the-clock care at this point. I hired two nurses from an outside agency. Each would do a twelve-hour shift. The hospice people were fine, but they weren't there all the time.

My money worries increased. My father's pension was no more. Besides the monthly rent at the Place, there were now these two nurses. There was her medication, and there were all these supplies she needed, now that she accepted her incontinence: bed pads, Depends, extra pads to wear *inside* the Depends, latex gloves for the nurses, Ensure, baby wipes, bed bath wipes, baby powder, diaper ointment, room freshener. We were blowing through my parents' scrimpings at breakneck speed: about $14,000 a month, none of which was covered by insurance.

A couple of weeks into the around-the-clock care, hospice, etc. I went to see my mother at the Place, filled with dread, fearing the worst.

Instead, she was sitting on the couch with one of the private nurses, a middle-aged woman from Jamaica named Goodie. She was fully dressed. She was wearing shoes. She was eating a tuna sandwich.

I knew that her retreat from the abyss should have filled me with joy, or at least relief. However, what I felt when I saw her was closer to:

Where, in the five Stages of Death, is **EAT TUNA SANDWICH?!?!?**

I had sort of adjusted to the idea that she was dying, and this was _throwing me off_.

Maybe if my mother and I had been close, I would have been thrilled to see her out of bed, chomping away. But we weren't. When I was growing up, one of her favorite argument-enders was: "I'm not your friend. I'm your mother." If you hear that enough times, it becomes hard to switch gears just because some years have gone by.

My mother was no longer my enemy when I grew up, but that didn't make her my friend. She was, as she insisted, my _mother_, plain and simple.

I was aware that she loved me. But something was off. I knew this before I could speak. My mother told me that as a baby, I cried a lot. That I didn't like to sleep, and that I didn't like to eat. I was born a month premature, by cesarean section, because of something related to the first baby: she was told by her obstetrician that if she carried me to term, her "uterus would rupture." At birth, I had poor muscle tone. The doctors told my mother I had a "congenital hip deformity," so she had to bring me back to the hospital every few months for x-rays. I didn't walk until I was 18 months old - about half a year later than average.

It was determined that there was nothing wrong with me. Nevertheless, I was probably not a fun baby. I had one cold after another, and from the time I could speak, one anxiety after another. I was my father's daughter, not my mother's. I can sympathize with her desire to leave me in the care of someone else for a while, although who knows what I thought back then.

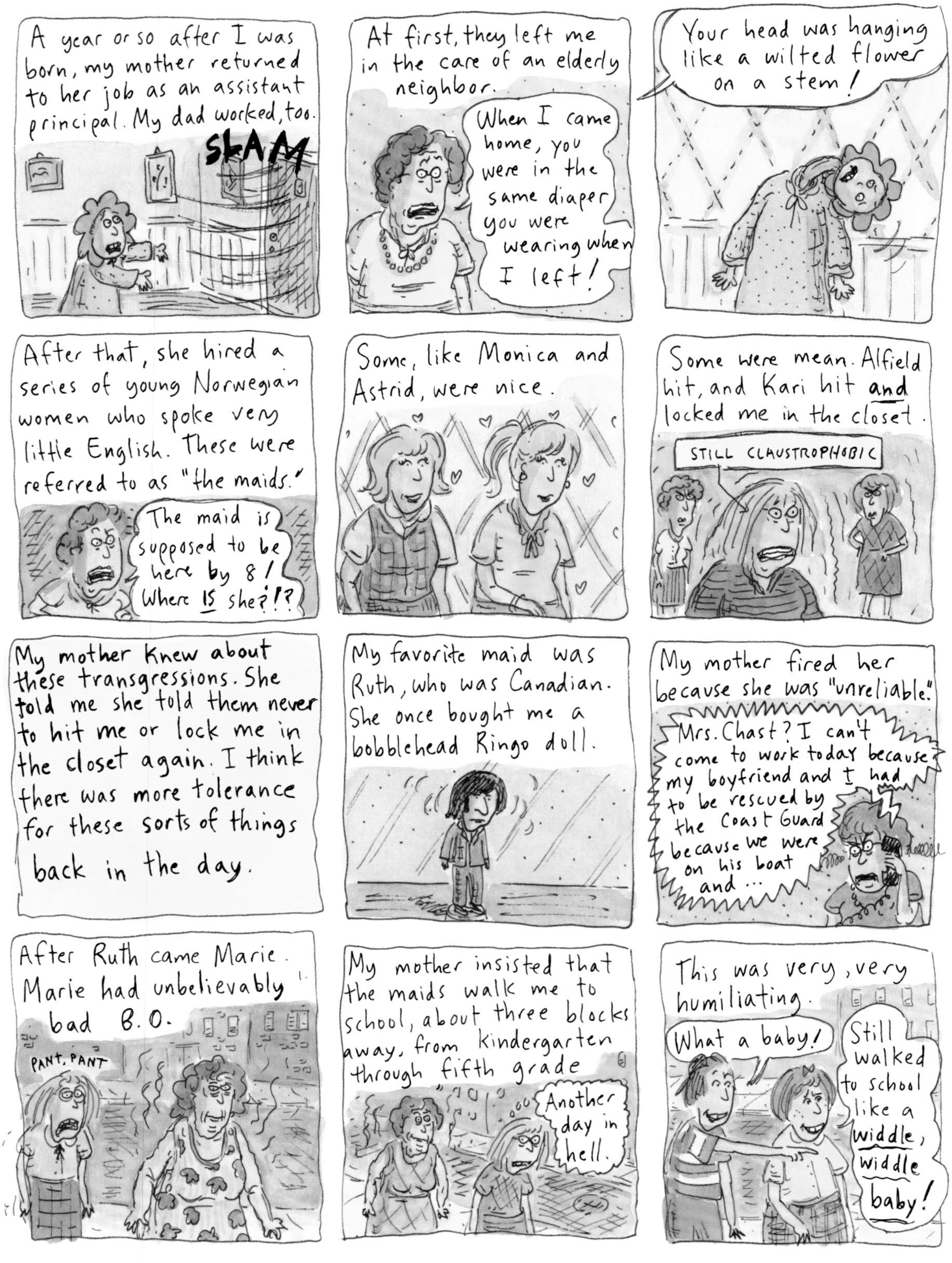

A year or so after I was born, my mother returned to her job as an assistant principal. My dad worked, too.
SLAM
At first, they left me in the care of an elderly neighbor.
When I came home, you were in the same diaper you were wearing when I left!
Your head was hanging like a wilted flower on a stem!
After that, she hired a series of young Norwegian women who spoke very little English. These were referred to as "the maids."
The maid is supposed to be here by 8! Where IS she?!?
Some, like Monica and Astrid, were nice.
Some were mean. Alfield hit, and Kari hit and locked me in the closet.
STILL CLAUSTROPHOBIC
My mother knew about these transgressions. She told me she told them never to hit me or lock me in the closet again. I think there was more tolerance for these sorts of things back in the day.
My favorite maid was Ruth, who was Canadian. She once bought me a bobblehead Ringo doll.
My mother fired her because she was "unreliable."
Mrs. Chast? I can't come to work today because my boyfriend and I had to be rescued by the Coast Guard because we were on his boat and ...
After Ruth came Marie. Marie had unbelievably bad B.O.
PANT, PANT
My mother insisted that the maids walk me to school, about three blocks away, from kindergarten through fifth grade
Another day in hell.
This was very, very humiliating.
What a baby!
Still walked to school like a widdle, widdle baby!

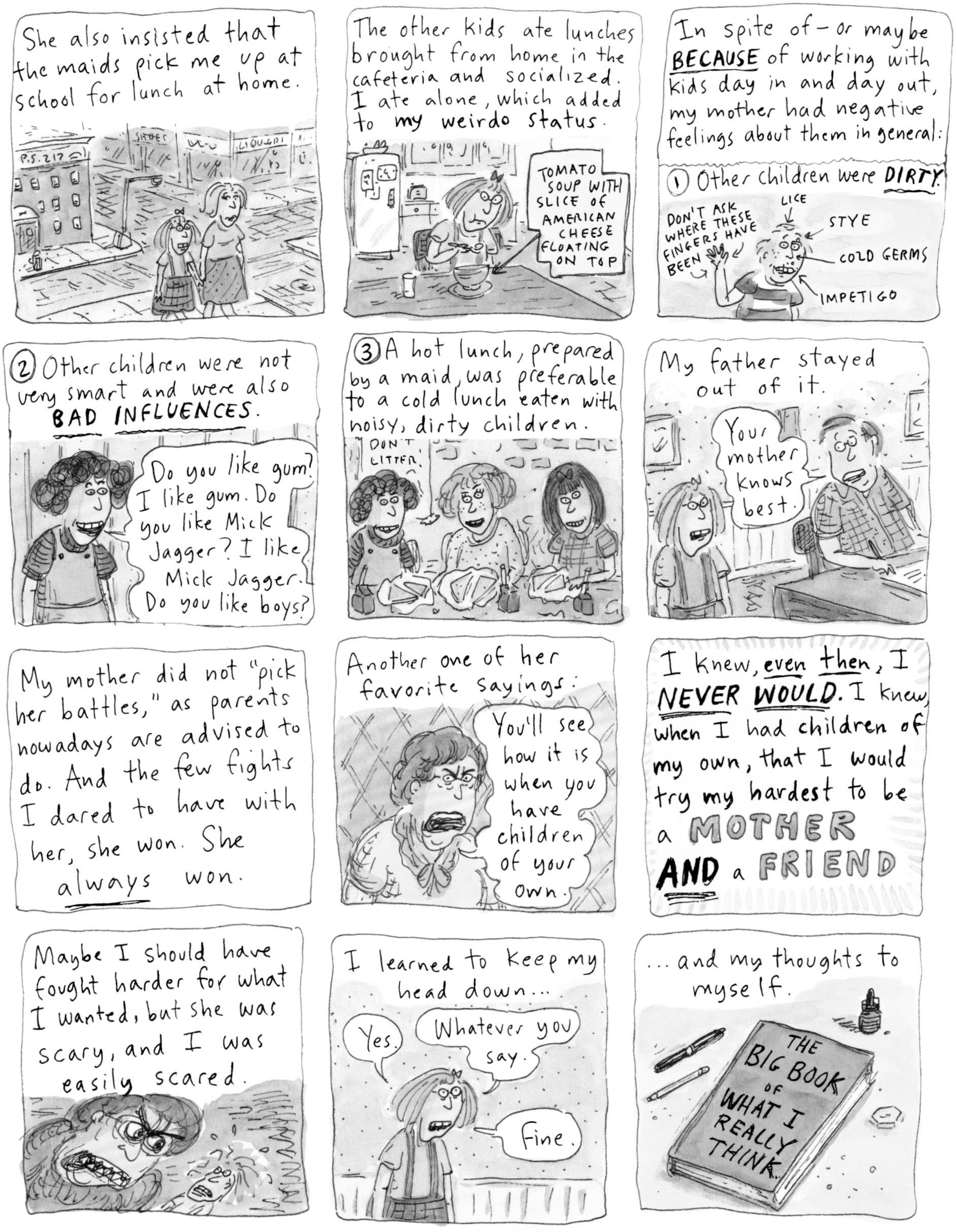
She also insisted that the maids pick me up at school for lunch at home.
P.S. 217
The other kids ate lunches brought from home in the cafeteria and socialized. I ate alone, which added to my weirdo status.
TOMATO SOUP WITH SLICE OF AMERICAN CHEESE FLOATING ON TOP
In spite of—or maybe BECAUSE of working with kids day in and day out, my mother had negative feelings about them in general:
1 Other children were DIRTY.
DON'T ASK WHERE THESE FINGERS HAVE BEEN
LICE
STYE
COLD GERMS
IMPETIGO
2 Other children were not very smart and were also BAD INFLUENCES.
Do you like gum? I like gum. Do you like Mick Jagger? I like Mick Jagger. Do you like boys?
3 A hot lunch, prepared by a maid, was preferable to a cold lunch eaten with noisy, dirty children.
DON'T LITTER
My father stayed out of it.
Your mother knows best.
My mother did not "pick her battles," as parents nowadays are advised to do. And the few fights I dared to have with her, she won. She always won.
Another one of her favorite sayings:
You'll see how it is when you have children of your own.
I knew, even then, I NEVER WOULD. I knew, when I had children of my own, that I would try my hardest to be a MOTHER AND a FRIEND
Maybe I should have fought harder for what I wanted, but she was scary, and I was easily scared.
I learned to keep my head down...
Yes.
Whatever you say.
Fine.
...and my thoughts to myself.
THE BIG BOOK OF WHAT I REALLY THINK

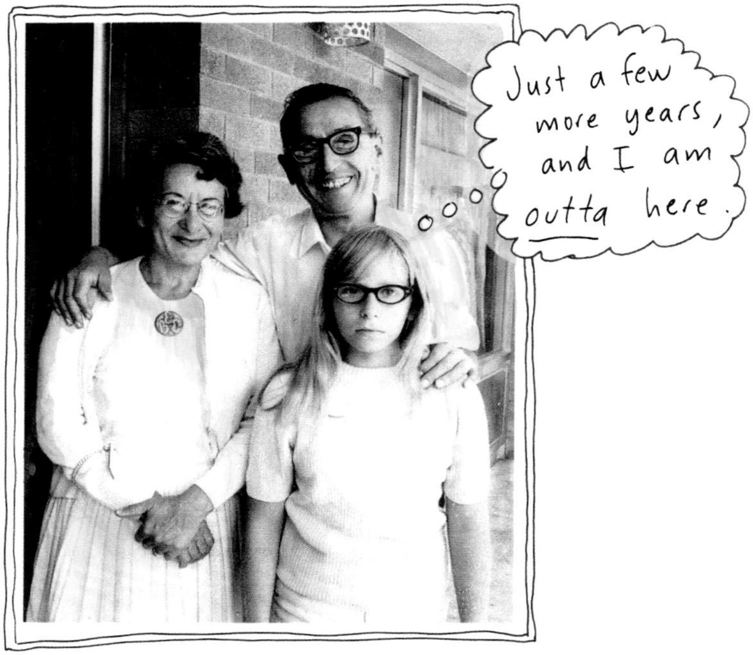
Just a few more years, and I am outta here.

Me at 12.

BEDTIME STORIES

In less than two months by January of 2009, my mother regained the fifteen pounds she'd lost. She didn't go to the dining room, but she was eating. And when she didn't eat, the aides made sure she drank Ensure. I remembered what one of the hospice people called the aides who supplied these nutritional drinks: human feeding tubes.

◄ ～ A D V E R T I S E M E N T ～ ◆ ►

WAAAH! Grandma's 108 and doesn't want to eat any more!

She's throwing in the TOWEL!

I wish there was something I could give her so she could LIVE FOREVER!

Say there! Have you ever heard of Ensure®?

No! What's in it?

Let's see: water, sugar (sucrose), corn maltodextrin, milk protein concentrate, soy oil, canola oil, soy protein concentrate, corn oil, potassium citrate, natural and artificial flavor, magnesium phosphate, sodium citrate, soy lecithin, calcium phosphate, magnesium chloride, salt, choline chloride, ascorbic acid, carrageenan, potassium chloride, ferrous sulfate, dl-alpha-tocopheryl acetate, zinc sulfate, niacinamide, calcium pantothenate, manganese sulfate, cupric sulfate, vitamin a palmitate, thiamine chloride hydrochloride, pyridoxine hydrochloride, riboflavin, folic acid, chromium chloride, biotin, sodium molybdate, potassium iodide, sodium selenate, phylloquinone, vitamin D3 and cyanocobalamin.

All's I know is, give her a few of these a day, and YOU MIGHT GET YOUR WISH!

She no longer qualified for hospice, but she still needed around-the-clock care. She couldn't feed, toilet, or dress herself. She could stay in the Place, as long as I hired private nurses, or I'd have to put her in a nursing home. Financially, it was a wash.

Goodie volunteered to do both shifts - to sleep in my mother's room, on the sofa. I wanted to buy her a bed, but she said the sofa was o.k. We worked out the payments. It was a phenomenal expense, but it was a phenomenal job. And she and my mother had BONDED. My mother had surrendered control to a lovely stranger.

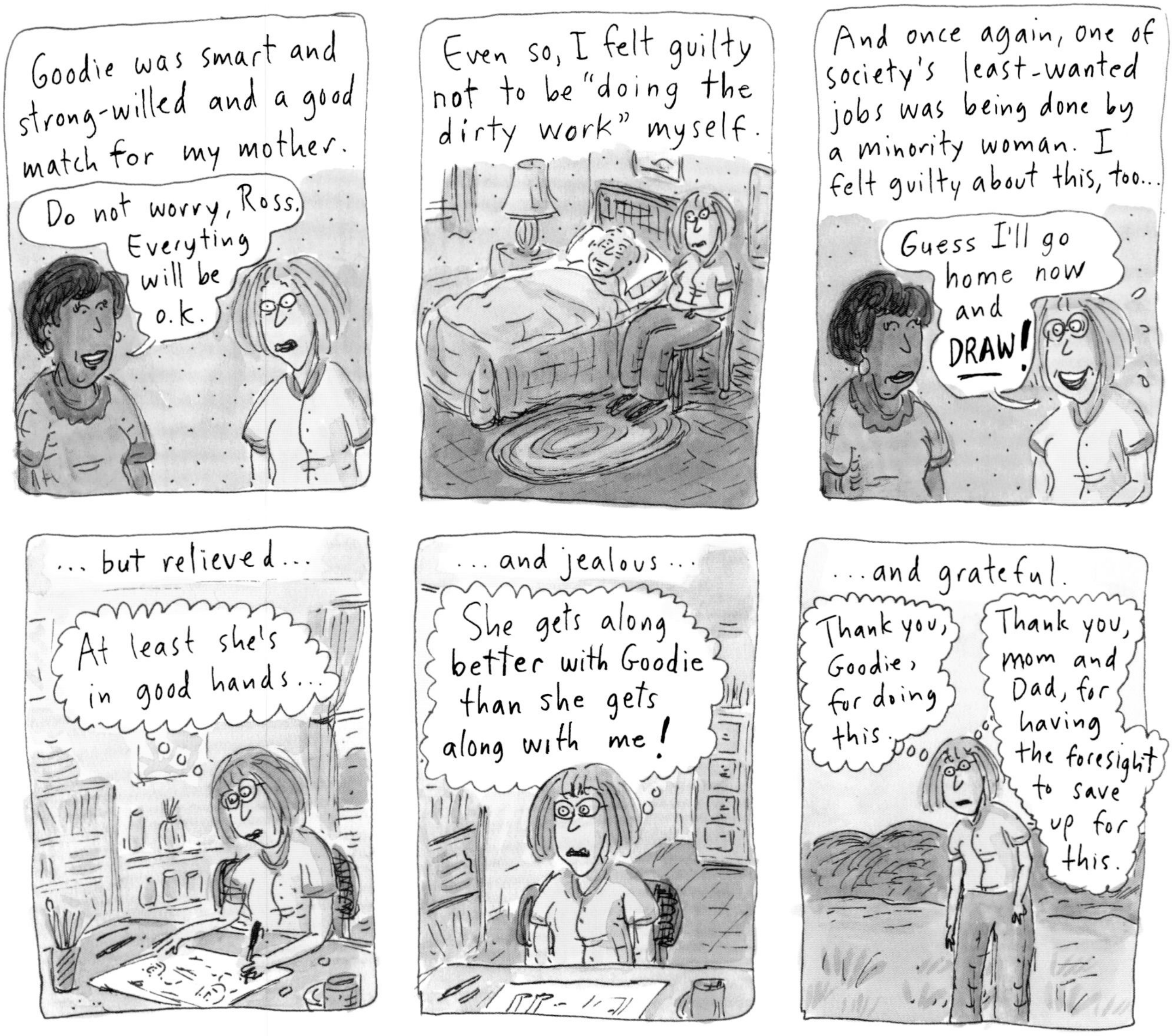
Goodie was smart and strong-willed and a good match for my mother.
Do not worry, Ross. Everyting will be o.k.
Even so, I felt guilty not to be "doing the dirty work" myself.
And once again, one of society's least-wanted jobs was being done by a minority woman. I felt guilty about this, too...
Guess I'll go home now and DRAW!
... but relieved...
At least she's in good hands...
... and jealous...
She gets along better with Goodie than she gets along with me!
... and grateful.
Thank you, Goodie, for doing this.
Thank you, mom and Dad, for having the foresight to save up for this.

My mother's drain-circling had slowed. But she was still completely incontinent, still slept a great deal, and was pretty much holed up in the room with Goodie. Also, her brains _were_ starting to melt:

I remembered seeing my uncle's discolored nail as a kid and being fascinated and repelled by it. It was odd to recognize it in this story. At least the meaning was - I think - positive: she felt close to Goodie. And Goodie wasn't bothered by it. She'd seen senile dementia before. Sometimes we exchanged "looks" during my mother's increasingly strange stories, like these:

DEAD DAD

Your father died before you were born - when I was pregnant with you.

My father, Harry, said he would buy me a house, and he would live with us and baby-sit you while I was at work.

Mom, that's not true.

Yes, it is. AND **I** SHOULD _KNOW_!

ASS FULL OF BUCK-SHOT

There was a break-in at the Place! All the men were moved over to the women's side.

I shot the intruder with my BB gun. I gave him an ass full of buckshot!

I'd like to stand him on a stage, pull down his pants, and take out the pellets one by one in front of everybody!

UNUSUAL ADOPTION

Did I ever tell you about how the Miltons got Paula?

They went out shopping, and when they got back to their car, there was a grocery bag leaning against the wheel...

...and inside the bag was a baby!

As the year continued, she spent more and more time in bed. The stories got stranger and stranger.

I started to get really fascinated by these "waking dreams," and looked forward to the next one. And, of course, I was writing them down.

Many of my mother's stories involved my father's mother — my grandmother — Katie. They had not had a good relationship.

Katie came from Russia in one of the great waves of immigration around 1900, like all my grandparents.

She lived across the street from us throughout my childhood in a walk-up that had become pretty much a tenement.

Her husband, William, died before I was born.

COLOR-BLIND HOUSE PAINTER

SWEET PERSON

COMMUNIST

SMOKED A LOT

DRANK

DIED OF A HEART ATTACK IN HIS 50s

Katie was contemptuous of William and made him sleep in a tiny, rubbish-filled room.

Go.

But she **ADORED** my father, her only child.

Georgelah, if you don't get all A's, I go jump out the window, mein darling.

When my father and mother got married, Katie never forgave either of them.

She died in 1972. In a Place.

My parents'
college
graduation
photos

Me, age 1

My mother's
mother, Mollie

My father's
mother, Katie, the
imaginary
murderer

OLD-COUNTRY GRANDMAS

FUN FACTS:

1. When my mother was a child, she had diptheria. She had a "web of mucus" which grew across her throat. Mollie, ever resourceful, took a clean rag, wrapped it around her finger, and "ripped the web out."

2. Katie slept at the foot of my father's bed, crosswise, until the day he married.

3. Mollie believed that people on TV could see her.

4. The floors of Katie's apartment were covered in wall-to-wall sheets of newspaper. Always. My parents had no explanation for this.

KATIE STORIES

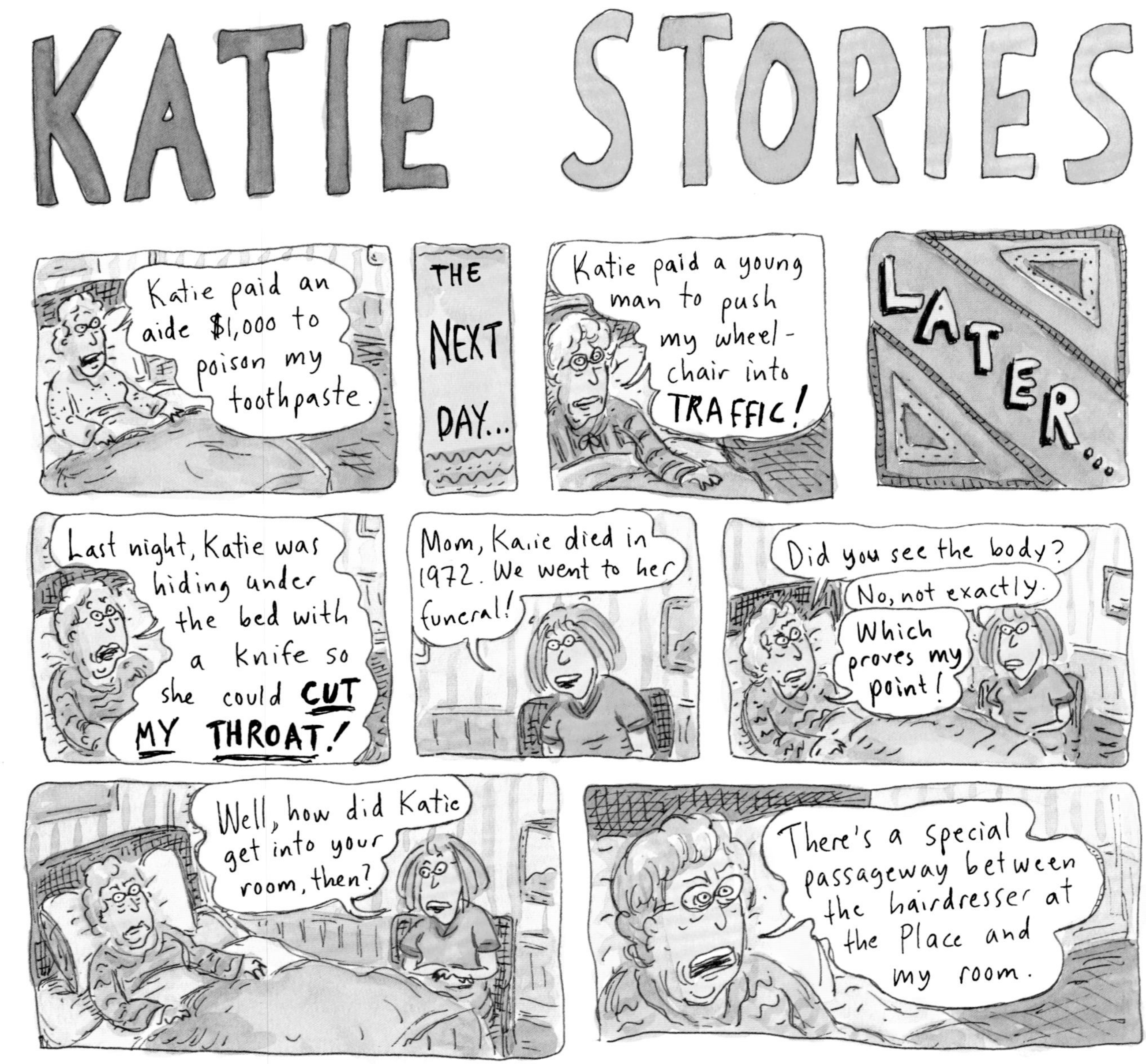
Katie paid an aide $1,000 to poison my toothpaste.
THE NEXT DAY...
Katie paid a young man to push my wheel-chair into TRAFFIC!
LATER...
Last night, Katie was hiding under the bed with a knife so she could CUT MY THROAT!
Mom, Katie died in 1972. We went to her funeral!
Did you see the body?
No, not exactly.
Which proves my point!
Well, how did Katie get into your room, then?
There's a special passageway between the hairdresser at the Place and my room.

More stories, not about Katie:

She told me that her older brother, who had died a few years before, came to visit, and said that when she got to hell, he would "show her the ropes." I asked her why she thought she was going to hell, and she got a "why are you asking such a stupid question" look on her face. This may have had something to do with all the fire-and-brimstone preachers Goodie watched on the TV.

Stick with me, Liz.

She told me that her father asked her, "Who's your daddy?" and when she said, "You," he said, "No, your mother had an affair with the neighbor, and _he's_ your daddy."

Her father, Harry, had "stacks of $10,000 bills" hidden somewhere. I should try to find them.

Had I heard what happened last week? Goodie went to her car to get something, but she was gone such a long time that my mother started to worry. So she called the main desk at the Place. They asked, "What kind of car does Goodie drive," so my mother told them. And lo and behold: Goodie was under the car, unconscious, and frozen to the ice!!! A guy "from the kitchen" had followed her to her car and pushed her! The important thing is: my mother saved Goodie's life.

After Katie, the second-most-popular genre of these stories was my mother's secret real-estate holdings. She knew I'd had dreams of moving back to Manhattan, where I'd lived for many years before my kids were born. I think maybe this was her way of making those wishes come true.

APARTMENT #1

The Board of Education* gave me an apartment in their building.

Where is that?

550 Park Avenue!!!

Oh.

It's as **big as a ballroom**: the **entire first floor.** It can hold 100 people!

To have an apartment in that building, you have to be **a person** of authority.

When my brother Aaron** visits, he can stay there.

It has lots of windows, and a private bathroom!

✱ My mother had been an assistant principal in the N.Y.C. public school system for decades. When I was a kid, I often heard stories about "The Board of Ed."

✱✱ Aaron was my mother's deceased brother, who was visiting her a lot. Goodie said that when he "visited," she saw a shadow pass over the bed.

APARTMENT # 2

*** My old, beloved apartment, where I lived before I had children, was on West 73rd near Amsterdam Avenue.

Of all the stories, I liked this one the best:

Needless to say, I am 99.9999999% sure nothing like this ever happened.

CHRYSALIS

Around this time, a friend sent me a quote from <u>Swann's Way</u>.

"The process which had begun in her . . . was the great and general renunciation which old age makes in preparation for death, the chrysalis stage of life, which may be observed whenever life has been unduly prolonged; even in old lovers who have lived for one another with the utmost intensity of passion, and in old friends bound by the closest ties of mental sympathy, who after a certain year, cease to make the necessary journey, or even cross the street to see one another, cease to correspond, and know well that they will communicate no more in this world."

On April 3, 2009, my mother had a little 97th birthday celebration in her room. Goodie got her out of bed and dressed her and brushed her hair. My cousin and her husband came. My daughter came, and a friend of mine came. Plus me, plus Goodie.

She asked me, "Am I 100?" I told her no, she was 97. She wanted a Reuben sandwich. I got her one. She ate it.

Despite the Reuben, by May it looked as if her decline had, once again, begun in earnest. The flow of surreal stories had all but stopped. When I visited, she seemed very tired. She'd ask me about my husband or the kids, and then drift off.

She was sleeping a lot. She wasn't eating much. She'd wake up and Goodie would give her an Ensure, and she'd go back to sleep. However, even at this point, she looked disconcertingly sturdy. When my father was "at the end," he looked frail—almost skeletel. My mother looked... robust.

Back off, mister.

My mother was existing in a state of suspended animation. She was not living and not dying. She didn't watch TV, read, go outside, play the piano, socialize, or even get out of bed. She slept, drank Ensures, got cleaned by Goodie or some other aide, and went back to sleep.

Several times, I was called to her bedside because things had "taken a turn," but then they'd turn around. I knew people – strong, healthy, relatively young people – who had gotten sick in their 40s, 50s, and 60s and died within a year. So what was going on here?!? How much longer could this state last? And also, would I feel different about her slow, drawn-out passage into death if we had been closer? Would I have bought truckloads of extra-strength Ensure? What about her oft-spoken wish to not be a lump of "pulsating protoplasm"? And what about the money?

... which means that I get $$$$ poorer...

My parents wouldn't have wanted that! Surely they didn't intend for their entire scrimpings to be used in this way!!!

Every month she stays alive, the Place and Goodie get $$$$ richer...

On the other hand, maybe it's different when death is near. Then it's LIFE AT ALL COSTS. And it's their money...

Ugh ugh ugh ugh ugh.

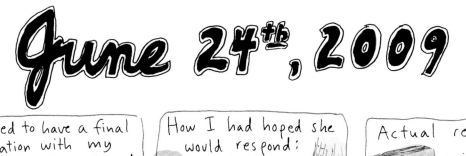
June 24th, 2009

I wanted to have a final conversation with my mother about the past, and finally worked up the courage to say something.

I wish we could have been better friends when I was growing up.

How I had hoped she would respond:

Me, too.

Actual response:

Does it worry you?

No... Does it worry YOU?

No.

Do you want me to stay, or should I go?

It doesn't matter.

It was time to go.

I left her room. Walked through the tasteful lobby of the Place as if everything was fine. Walked to my car. When I got in, I cried. The bellowing quality of the sobbing and the depth of the sadness I felt surprised me. I was angry, too. Why hadn't she tried harder to know me?

But I knew: if there had ever been a time in my relationship with my mother for us to get to know one another – and that's a very big "if" – that time had long since passed.

THE END

In mid-July, my mother's doctor decided it was time for her to go back into hospice care. This was not, as I had hoped, instead of Goodie's 24-hour care, but in addition to it. Her life was much like an infant's: mostly sleeping, with occasional wake-ups for Ensure or a few sips of ginger ale. Goodie would clean her and diaper her, and then my mother would go back to sleep. Sometimes she'd get a sponge bath in bed. She was done with talking, at least to me. Once, Goodie told me she requested some ice cream. When I visited, she was usually asleep, but occasionally, she'd open her eyes for a few seconds, see me, smile, and then go back to sleep.

There were a few "turns for the worse," but then things would settle down. A staff person told me she was praying for God to take her.

Hospice knew how stressed-out I was getting. Every time the phone rang, I felt a wave of panic. They gave me two "worry stones" that had been painted by volunteers.

(APPROX. ACTUAL SIZE)

I often asked the hospice volunteers about my mother's condition—how much longer did they think she would hold on?

One of the hospice ladies told me, "The Devil doesn't want her, and God's not ready." Another told me that she had never, in her entire time as a hospice volunteer, seen anything like my mother's tenacity.

Hospice also arranged for a Reiki therapist to come to my house. I guess they knew when the family of their "client" was getting sort of wacky. They'd probably seen it before and knew the signs. The therapist, who was a very, very short middle-aged woman, told me to sit. She then cupped my head in her hands for about three minutes. Then she put one hand on each shoulder and left them there for about two minutes. Her hands were very warm. Then one hand on my head, then one on shoulder. Head, shoulder. Head. Shoulder. This whole thing took about half an hour. It was supposed to relax me and help my "energy flow."

It didn't feel bad, but it didn't make me stop worrying.

A nurse at the Place put a DNR bracelet on my mother's wrist, to make sure that if she were suddenly taken to the hospital, no one would hook her up to a machine that would turn her into the dreaded "pulsating piece of protoplasm."

LIMITED TIME OFFER!

NOT AVAILABLE IN STORES!

GET THE ENTIRE ENSEMBLE!

But it depressed her to look at it all the time, which made sense to me. It was a little too close to a toe tag. I clipped it off and taped it to her medical file, which would go with her to the hospital. Hopefully.

THE LAST THINGS

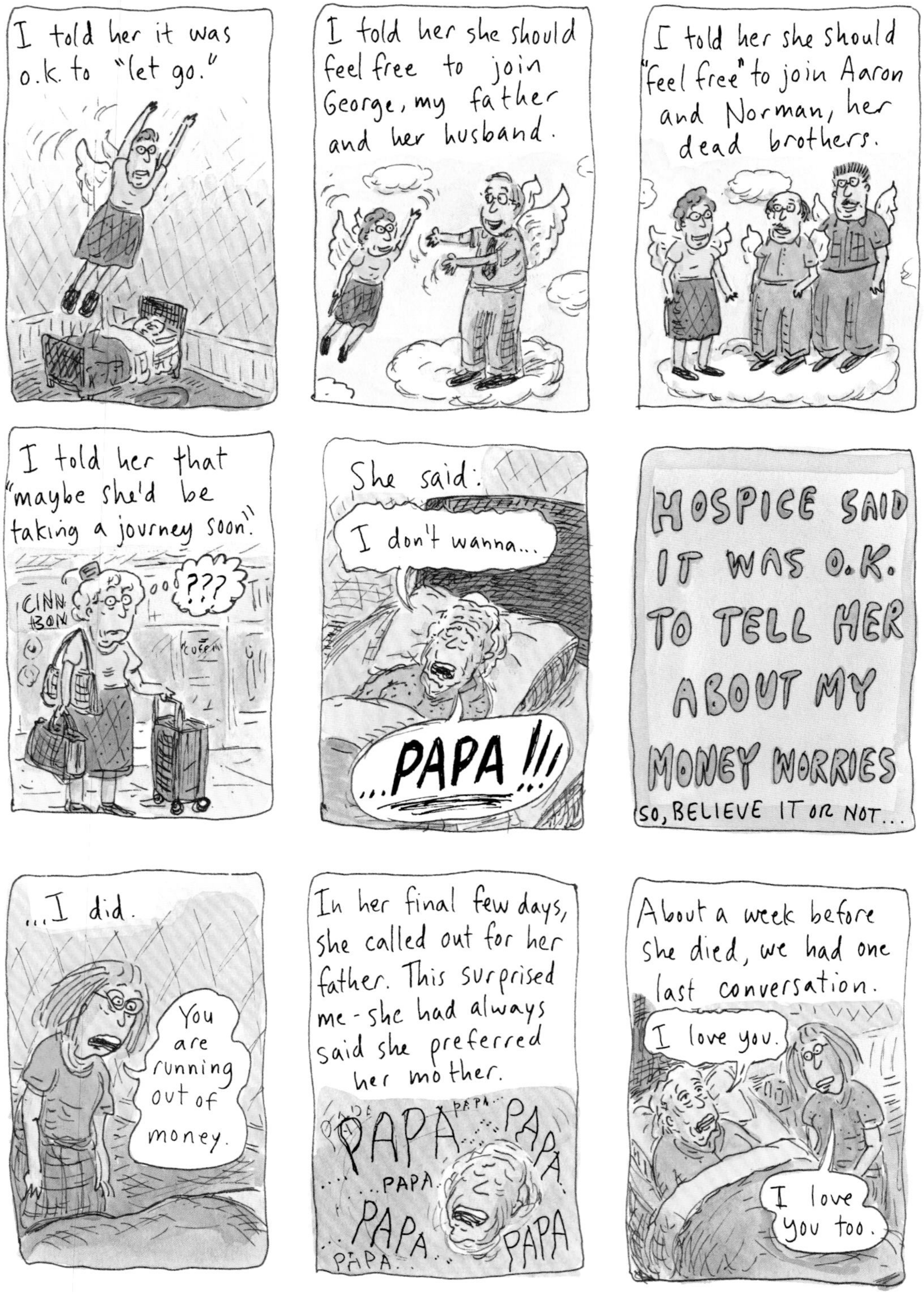
I told her it was o.k. to "let go."
I told her she should feel free to join George, my father and her husband.
I told her she should "feel free" to join Aaron and Norman, her dead brothers.
I told her that "maybe she'd be taking a journey soon."
CINNABON
COFFEE
???
She said:
I don't wanna...
...PAPA!!!
HOSPICE SAID IT WAS O.K. TO TELL HER ABOUT MY MONEY WORRIES
SO, BELIEVE IT OR NOT...
...I did.
You are running out of money.
In her final few days, she called out for her father. This surprised me - she had always said she preferred her mother.
PAPA
PAPA...
PAPA
PAPA
PAPA
PAPA
PAPA
PAPA
About a week before she died, we had one last conversation.
I love you.
I love you too.

My mother's condition was no better and maybe slightly worse at the beginning of September 2009. It was hard to tell. She didn't talk, she barely opened her eyes. She slept. How long could a person stay alive like this? No one seemed to know. Hospice stopped making guesses.

On September 27, my mother developed a hole which came through the skin on the surface of her abdomen. It was a direct result of her chronic diverticulosis. It was covered with a bandage. I asked Goodie to remove the bandage because I did not want to turn away from what was happening. The hole was about 1/4 inches in diameter, and it was reddish and inflamed at the edges. More shocking: the stool was coming out. She was not in pain - she was taking a significant amount of morphine at this point. I stroked her forehead and once I saw her eyeballs roll back in her head.

Hospice arranged for an oxygen tank to be brought into my mother's room in case her breathing worsened.

I was at home on Wednesday, September 30th at 8:15 P.M. when the phone rang. Goodie was on the line. It was time. I drove to the Place and got there at 8:35. My mother had died at 8:28. When I got there, she was in bed, in her pajamas. Her mouth was slightly open. She was still warm, but starting to turn yellowish.

Goodie left the room to fetch the people that one fetches when someone at the Place dies. While Goodie was gone, I was alone with my mother's body for a while. I drew her. I didn't know what else to do. I had been drawing her all summer, since the conversations had been reduced to almost nothing.

Goodie came back with a nurse and some staff people. The funeral director came with some people. They put her in a maroon corduroy bag and zipped it up. Then they took her away, and she was gone.

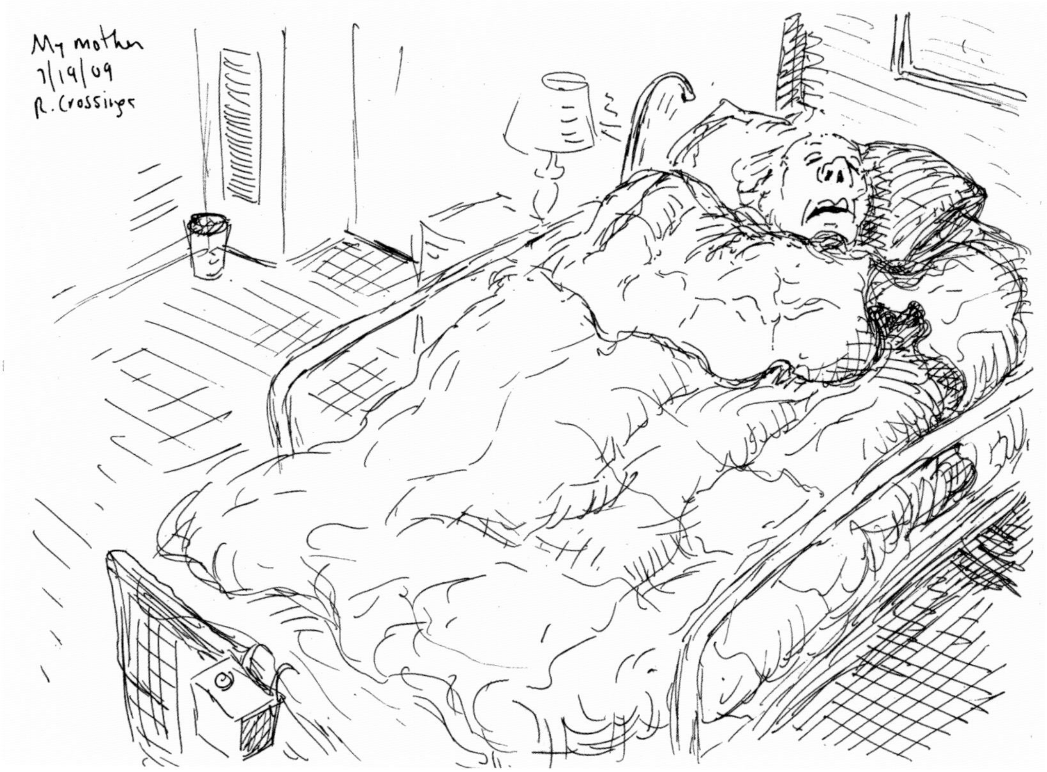
My mother
7/19/09
R. Crossinger

She raised her
eyebrows
suddenly

intense frowning

8/09

213

My mother— her mouth slack— down at
the corners

My mother
8/10/09

215

8/16/09

8/16/09

217

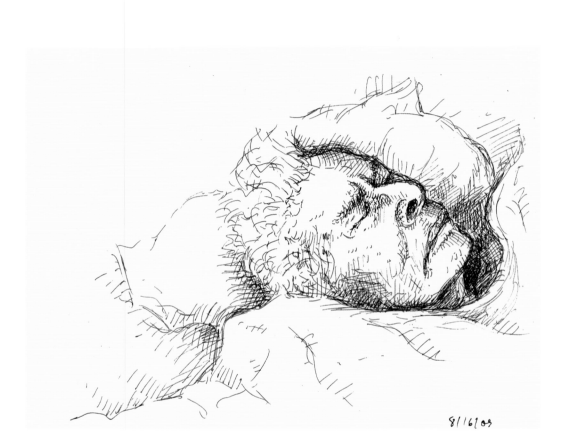

8/16/03

9/13/09

9/19/09

9/26/09

My mother died tonight
at 8:28

EPILOGUE

On the floor of my closet, along with shoes, old photo albums, wrapping paper, a sewing machine, a shelf of sleep t-shirts, an iron, a carton of my kids' childhood artwork, and some other miscellaneous stuff, are two special boxes.

One holds my father's cremains. The other holds my mother's.

My father's box is inside a navy blue velvet drawstring bag, which I placed inside of the ancient Channel 13 bag that he took everywhere.

My mother's box is inside a maroon velvet drawstring bag. It is "en plein air."

The funeral director had asked me if I wanted their ashes to be mixed together.

I told him that my mother had been so dominant when they were alive I thought it better if he had a little space of his own. Still close, but independent.

No, thanks.

mints

tissues

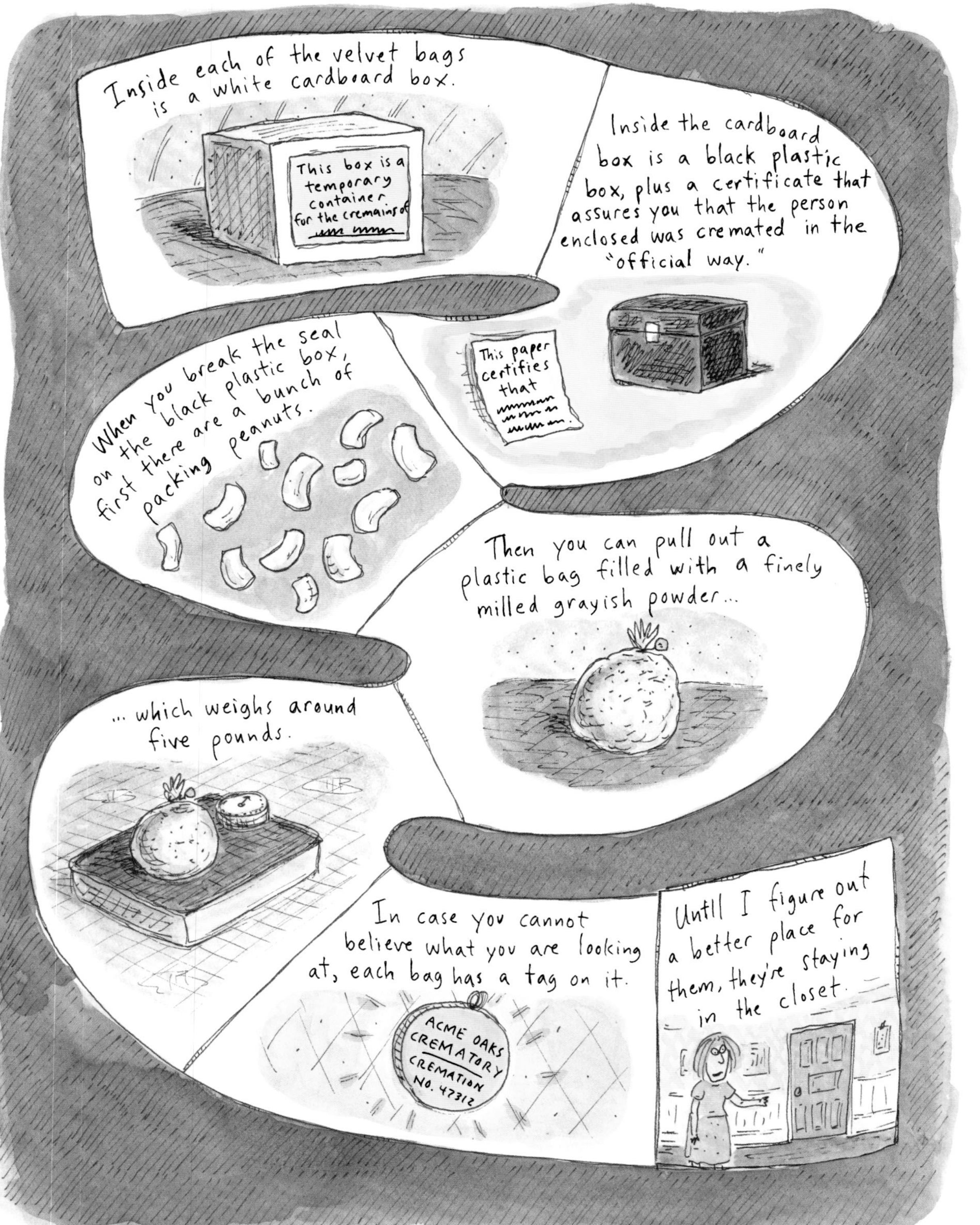

Inside each of the velvet bags is a white cardboard box.
This box is a temporary container for the cremains of
Inside the cardboard box is a black plastic box, plus a certificate that assures you that the person enclosed was cremated in the "official way."
This paper certifies that
When you break the seal on the black plastic box, first there are a bunch of packing peanuts.
Then you can pull out a plastic bag filled with a finely milled grayish powder...
...which weighs around five pounds.
In case you cannot believe what you are looking at, each bag has a tag on it.
ACME OAKS CREMATORY
CREMATION NO. 47312
Until I figure out a better place for them, they're staying in the closet.

I like having my parents in my closet. The thought of burying their cremains in an arbitrary hole in the ground does not appeal to me. We don't have a family plot, so choosing one cemetery over another seems random. Throwing their ashes off the side of a boat makes as much sense to me as tossing them in a wastebasket at Starbucks. And decanting them into a decorative urn placed on the mantelpiece in the living room is just... ugh.

My bedroom closet is not large. The clothes in it are not stylish, but they are organized by color in a way I like to look at. The shoes are on a tree, or placed in pairs on the floor. It's not a super-neat closet, but it's not messy. I think it makes a nice home for them. Every time I open its door, I see the boxes, and I think of them.

Even though he often drove me bats, I remember my dad with great affection. In my heart of hearts, I feel as if he and I were kindred spirits. I'm still working things out with my mother. Sometimes, I want to go back in time and warn her: "Don't do that! If you're mean to her (me) again, you'll lose her trust forever! It's not worth it!!!" Obviously, I can't.

Maybe when I completely give up this desire to make it right with my mother, I'll know what to do with their cremains. Or, maybe not.

For as far back as I can remember, I felt far outside my parents' duo. There were many times, from when I was a little girl until just a couple of weeks ago, that I was sure I was adopted. I have to admit, though: if they had adopted me, they had done a sensational job of covering their tracks. Adoptees or not, they were my one and only set of parents, and now they are gone, a fact that feels indescribably strange, even four and six years after their deaths. They still appear in my dreams. In the ones with my mother, I usually am about to go somewhere with my friends or my husband or my kids, but suddenly, she begins to collapse and I have to take care of her. My father usually appears sitting at our kitchen counter, drinking tea, and reading the newspaper, and he is not worried.

Roz Chast.
June 17, 2013